To Grandad

Happy Birthday 95

Naomi + Keith
x x   x x

THE
CUCKOO LINE

Near Mayfield.

O. J. Morris, courtesy E. Jackson

THE
CUCKOO LINE

ALAN ELLIOTT

WILD SWAN PUBLICATIONS LTD.

I1X 4—4—2T No. 2002 leaving Hailsham with the 1.50 p.m. Tunbridge Wells to Eastbourne train on 12th May 1951.   *S. C. Nash*

Designed by Paul Karau
Typesetting by Berkshire Publishing Services
Printed by Amadeus Press, Huddersfield

Published by
WILD SWAN PUBLICATIONS LTD.
1-3 Hagbourne Road, Didcot, Oxon, OX11 8DP

ACKNOWLEDGEMENTS

So many people have given help and encouragement in the production of this book that it is inevitable that some names will be omitted from the list. My apologies, therefore, are offered to those who have not been mentioned and my sincere thanks go to all who have contributed in any way.

Particular thanks must go to the staff of various organisations such as the Chief Civil Engineer's Department, British Rail (Southern Region), The Public Records Office at Kew, the Newspaper Library at Collindale, the British Museum Map Room, East Sussex County Library, the Public Records Office at Lewes, East Sussex, and also Kent County Library.

Thanks are also due to John Minnis, Mike Crittenden, Arch Overbury, Peter Hay and other members of the Brighton Circle who have, between them, provided photographs and information, and checked manuscripts. The Signalling Record Society and the Southern Railways Group provided many detailed signalling diagrams and historical notes. Paul Ellis and Michael Jessop of the Heathfield Model Railway Club, with their local knowledge, were able to provide first hand information on the area.

The response to my requests for photographs was quite incredible and I must thank Dr. Ian C. Allen, R. C. Riley, S. C. Nash, John Scrace, A. E. Bennett, J. H. Meredith, H. C. Casserley, Brian Hart and R. G. Spalding as well as Lens of Sutton and the Hailsham History and Natural History Society for the provision of so many interesting and informative pictures.

Anne Penfield, who has worked with me long enough to understand my scribbled handwriting deserves particular thanks for the many hours she spent typing and re-typing from my manuscript. So also does Grant Alderson who gave valuable assistance with the proof reading.

Finally, mention must be made of my wife, Mary, who has put up with rooms scattered with papers and drawings and household jobs left undone, my daughter, Sandra, who has drawn the maps and my daughter Jennifer who also did some of the typing and has checked page proofs.

Alan Elliott

CONTENTS

INTRODUCTION

In the early days of the railway age, lines were built simply to create or fulfil a need and to make a profit, but by the second half of the nineteenth century most of the main routes had been established and the well-known companies of the pre-grouping era had emerged. These companies virtually monopolised the areas in which they operated and it was to protect those monopolies that many new lines were being proposed in order to fill up the country and prevent other companies from encroaching upon the territory. Three railway companies competed for traffic in the south-east and one of them, the London, Brighton & South Coast Railway, monopolised the triangular area formed by London, Hastings and Portsmouth. The South Eastern Railway and the London, Chatham & Dover Railway, however, very nearly ruined each other competing for the traffic between London and Dover, and throughout Kent, until they were forced by financial circumstances to form a combined management committee in 1899 under the title of South Eastern and Chatham Railway. In addition to the cut-throat competition for the Dover traffic, both companies made repeated attempts to invade Brighton territory in order to tap the lucrative traffic from Brighton and Eastbourne.

This book begins with an attempt to portray a line which, although nominally independent at the outset, owed its existence to both the offensive attitude of the SER and the defensive stance of the LBSCR, and, although the line became a part of the Brighton company's network, the victory really belonged to the South Eastern Railway. To show why this was so, Chapter One gives a brief history of the LBSCR and its territorial disputes in East Sussex, and the second chapter shows how the Brighton company was outmanoeuvred by the SER.

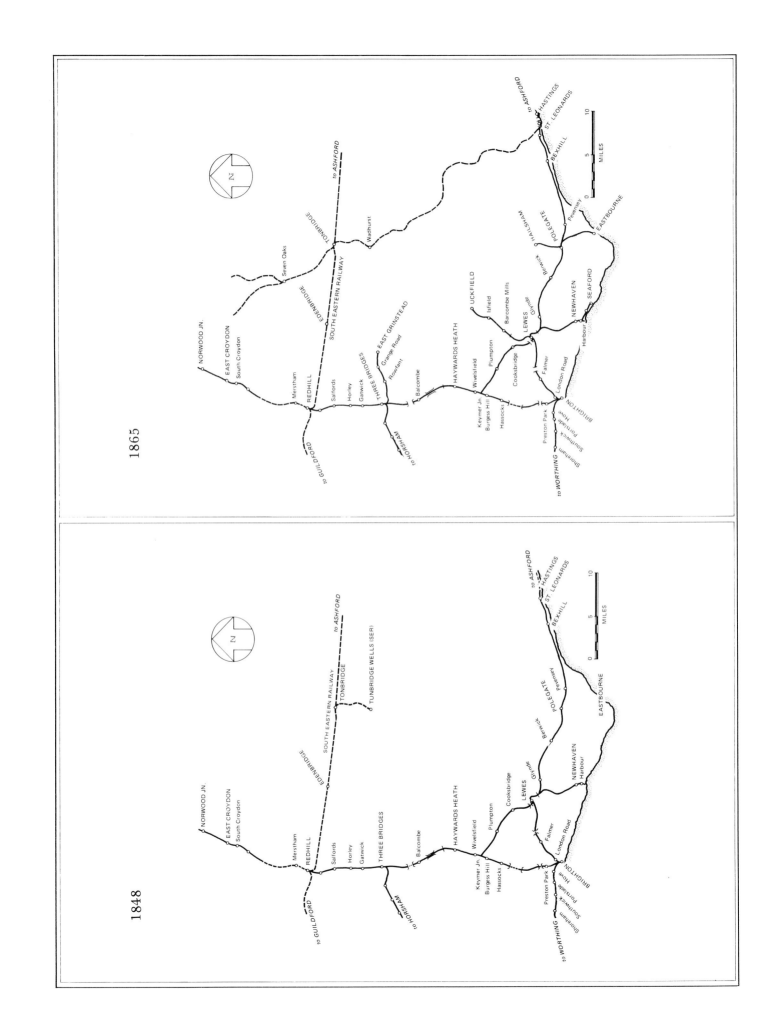

RAILWAY DEVELOPMENT IN EAST SUSSEX

'There were seven to eight trains running on these lines in one day now, whereas one horse bus and a fly was sufficient to suit the traffic before any line was made at all.'   Samuel Laing, 1867[1]

THE above remarks, uttered by the new chairman of the LBSCR, referred to the growing number of rural lines in Sussex. It must be remembered, however, that the history of these lines derived to a great extent from the efforts of the company to prevent encroachment upon its monopoly at Brighton and Eastbourne. The title of the company, The London, Brighton and South Coast Railway, accurately described its interest in the carriage of passengers and goods between London and the towns along the south coast between Portsmouth and Hastings. The most important of these towns was Brighton and the company can probably claim to have been the first line to have been built primarily to develop and serve a holiday resort. Brighton had been the resort of fashionable society led by the Prince Regent and in the ten years from 1821 the population grew from about 24,000 to about 40,000. This was largely due to the supposed medicinal properties of sea bathing and there were also large numbers of visitors attracted to the town. Thirty-six coaches were running daily between London and Brighton in 1836 and the approximate number of passengers carried during the previous year was 117,000. The average fare for the journey, which took about six hours, was twenty-one shillings for a seat inside and twelve shillings for travelling outside[2] and it is interesting to compare those prices with the train fares of a hundred years later. In 1937 a monthly return cost eight shillings and ninepence and a cheap day ticket could be bought for six shillings and sixpence. This, then, was the market that attracted the early railway promoters and when it was won it was well worth defending.

The first published proposals for a railway from London to Brighton were in 1823 but the Royal Assent was eventually given in 1837 for a direct line, with authority to construct branches to Shoreham, Lewes and Newhaven. The South Eastern Railway had been incorporated the year before with authority to build their line from London to Dover and the two companies were to share the line between London and Redhill. Parliament, in its wisdom, considered that one line into London, from the south, would be sufficient.

Brighton had been an aristocratic resort but it was not long before 'Society' began to give way to the middle and working classes, especially with the advent of the excursion train which was introduced on the Easter Monday of 1844. By 1845 monthly, quarterly and annual season tickets were being issued to encourage the London businessman to live in Brighton.

The real history of the London, Brighton and South Coast Railway, however, lies in the evolution of the lines in the triangles formed either side of the main line. In the first half of the nineteenth century the Weald of

Sussex was poor and backward,[3] there was no industry and farmers scratched a living from infertile soil. After catering for the wealthy commuters who, in the 1840s, still lived in the countryside around Penge and Sydenham, the railway cut right across the sparsely populated country to its profitable coastal resort. In 1846 the line from Brighton to Hastings via Lewes was opened and in the following year a loop was constructed from Keymer, near Hassocks on the main line, to Lewes allowing a direct route from London to Hastings. Also in 1847, a branch was constructed from Lewes to Newhaven and in 1849 two short branches from Polegate were opened. One of these went south to Eastbourne, with its population of about 3,000, and the other went north to the market town of Hailsham.

Soon after this the Brighton company lost its independent access to the ancient port of Hastings. Back in 1845 powers had been obtained to extend the Hastings line to Ashford, keeping close to the coast for most of the route but the South Eastern Railway deposited counter proposals in the shape of a branch from Headcorn to Hastings via Tenterden.[4] Parliament preferred the coastal route but was persuaded that it could be better worked by the SER and the powers were transferred to that company. The line was opened on Friday, 13th February, 1851, and on the same day the Brighton company opened a quarter of a mile extension from their station at St. Leonards to the new South Eastern station at Hastings. Trouble immediately flared up between the two companies and it was not until the Saturday that a few Brighton trains were allowed through. Two engines and seventeen coaches were then left at Hastings on the Sunday, ready for the Monday morning services. Early on the Monday the SER took up the track at the junction of the two companies' lines, stood a ballast train across the sidings at Hastings and marooned the Brighton agent in his office there. The LBSCR hired a bus but the SER erected a barrier across the station approach, thus preventing its departure. The Brighton company quickly obtained an injunction against the South Eastern and were able to run their trains again but it was not until 5th December 1870 that they were allowed to stop at the intermediate station at Warrior Square.[5]

A shorter South Eastern route to Hastings also had its beginnings in 1845, when a branch from Tonbridge to Tunbridge Wells was authorised. This branch was continued in stages until it finally reached Hastings on 1st February 1852, giving the SER a slightly shorter route to Hastings than that of the Brighton company. Up to 1860 only two other branch lines penetrated the country between the Brighton and South Eastern main lines and these were from Three Bridges to East Grinstead, opened in 1855, and from Lewes to Uckfield, opened in 1858.

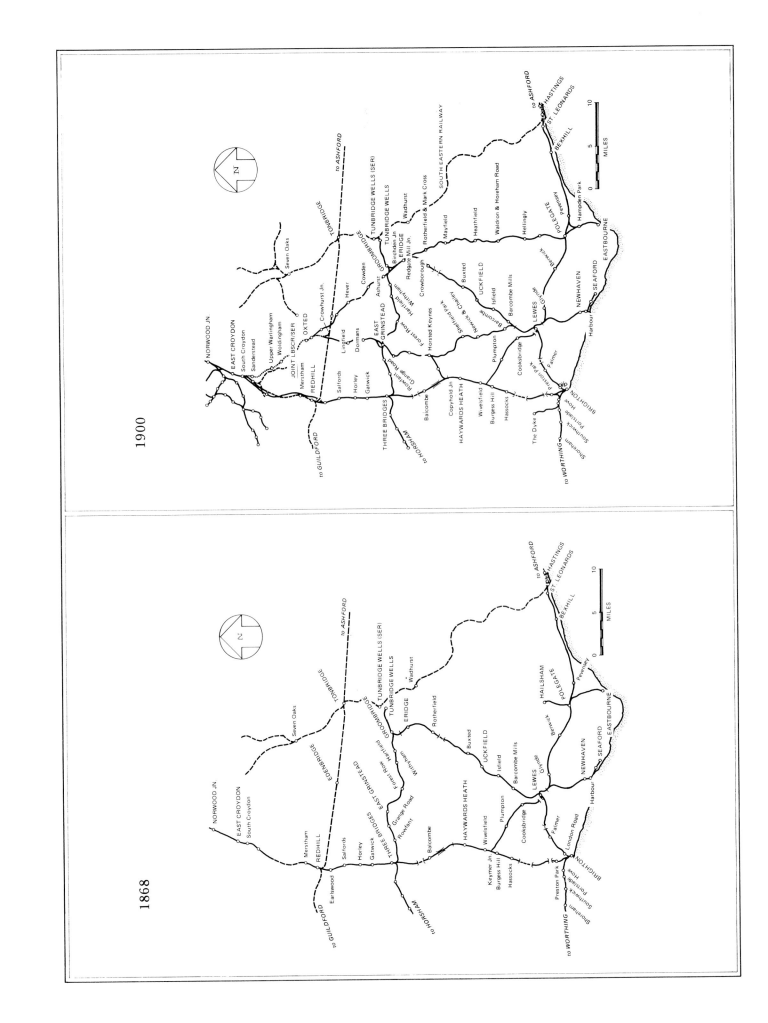

A Polegate and Hailsham local train at Eastbourne in 1868, hauled by London, Brighton & South Coast Railway Craven 0–4–2 tank locomotive No. 230.   *G. & R. Lavis*

The monopoly at Brighton faced a threat in 1863 when a private company, encouraged by the London, Chatham and Dover Railway, proposed building a line from London to Brighton through Beckenham, East Grinstead, Lewes and Kemp Town. The Bill was rejected by the Commons in that year and again in 1864, but it led to the LBSCR obtaining powers to construct lines to fill up the district. East Grinstead is thirteen miles and Uckfield is fifteen and a half miles from Tunbridge Wells and two private companies were incorporated to construct extensions to the existing branches which would meet at Groombridge and continue into Tunbridge Wells. The line from East Grinstead was opened in 1866 and that from Uckfield two years later but both companies were absorbed by the LBSCR before the lines opened.

It was now felt that Brighton was safe from encroachment but this was not the case at Eastbourne. In the same year as the Beckenham to Brighton proposal, a line from Croydon to Eastbourne was proposed by the South Eastern and in retaliation Brighton obtained powers to build the Ouse Valley Railway from Balcombe to Hailsham via Uckfield. In 1866, however, there was a national financial crisis and on 10th May the bankers Oferend and Gurnay, who were over-extended by £19 million, suspended business. The directors of the LBSCR thought they would be able to weather the storm and work started on the Ouse Valley line on 16th May and it continued for nine wasted months before being abandoned. The South Eastern had already been persuaded to withdraw its proposals in exchange for a short spur being built to connect the two companies' separate stations at Tunbridge Wells.

In 1865 it was the LBSCR who inspired a Surrey and Sussex Junction Railway to build a line from Croydon to Tunbridge Wells via Oxted and this so incensed the SER that they temporarily joined forces with the LCDR to obtain yet another Bill for a London, Lewes and Brighton Railway. The financial crisis of the following year also

killed this proposal as well as causing work on the Surrey and Sussex Junction Railway to be suspended.

Financial exhaustion of all the combatants ensured peace in the area until 1872, when a group of Eastbourne citizens made proposals for a railway to Tunbridge Wells but eight years were to pass and several schemes considered before the line was completed and then only after much intrigue. The link between the two stations at Tunbridge Wells was opened to goods traffic in 1867 and to passenger traffic in 1876. After the eventual opening of the Eastbourne to Tunbridge Wells line in 1880, warfare between the LBSCR and the SER began to peter out. Using the earthworks of the defunct Surrey and Sussex Junction Railway, a jointly owned line was opened in 1884 between Croydon and Crowhurst where a spur connected the line to the South Eastern's Redhill to Tonbridge route. Continuing on from Crowhurst, the line was exclusively Brighton owned to East Grinstead where it made an end-on junction with the Lewes to East Grinstead line which opened in 1882. The railway map was almost completed in 1888 with the opening of the Oxted to Groombridge line using the remaining section of the Surrey and Sussex Junction Railway's right of way. This section of line was also exclusively Brighton owned.

References

1. The Chairman of the LBSCR addressing a Special General Meeting in May 1867.
2. Dendy-Marshall, C. F. *History of the Southern Railway.*
3. There was a thriving iron industry in the Weald up to the end of the seventeenth century but it had ceased to exist by the end of the eighteenth century.
4. This line was completed as the Kent and East Sussex Light Railway in 1905.
5. White, H. P. *A Regional History of the Railways of Great Britain, Vol. 2.*

Eastbourne station c.1905 with 'B2' class No. 323 *William Cubitt* pulling away with the 'Sunny South Express'. Standing in one of the central roads is a Billinton 6-wheel saloon. The photographer has evidently managed to capture the slipping driving wheels for which these engines were notorious.

O. J. Morris Collection, courtesy John Minnis

CHAPTER TWO

EASTBOURNE TO TUNBRIDGE WELLS

'Our Brighton policy has always been to remain on the defensive. We do not want to make new lines.'

Samuel Laing, 22nd July, 1874.[1]

SAMUEL Laing had been a law clerk in the Railway Department of the Board of Trade when he was elected as chairman of the London, Brighton and South Coast Railway in 1848, and when he resigned in 1855 to go to India he left the company in a sound and prosperous position. Returning twelve years later, he found that the company was very nearly insolvent with the original capital of £7.7 million having been increased to nearly £18 million without a corresponding increase in net profits. Although passenger revenue had been increased by 60%, train mileages had increased by 170%[2] with too many unprofitable branch lines being built. Mr. Laing remained as chairman until 1896 and for nearly thirty years his policy was one of peace with the neighbouring companies and the avoidance of any additional competitive lines. Some new lines were forced upon the company, however, and the Tunbridge Wells and Eastbourne Railway in particular falls into this category.

There had been numerous schemes for railway lines in this area and various plans were deposited from 1856 onwards. A very detailed description of one route, which connected with the South Eastern line near Wadhurst, was published in 1863 but this differed considerably from deposited plans of the same date[3] and the first indication of the line which eventually came to be built came in December 1872 when the Tunbridge Wells and Eastbourne Railway was included in a list of new bills for the next Parliamentary Sesssion.[4]

Several weeks later, on Monday, 27th January 1873, the Eastbourne Ratepayers Association held one of their periodical meetings and at this meeting a Mr. Hassal asked if anyone could give him any information about the proposed new railway between their town and Tunbridge Wells. During the discussion that followed, great differences of opinion were expressed as to the benefits likely to accrue to the town if the line, as contemplated, were carried out. In reply to a comment that a more direct line might be desirable, a Mr. Cavendish said that he believed that a better line was contemplated but he would give no further information to the meeting.[5] Cavendish, being the family name of the Dukes of Devonshire, with their huge estates at Eastbourne, gives the first indication of the powerful interests backing this scheme.

Details of the project were reported on 1st February 1873.[6] It entailed the formation of an independent company to build 23 miles 3¼ chains of new railway commencing at one point by a junction with the East Grinstead, Groombridge and Tunbridge Wells line of the Brighton company, and terminating at the Hailsham station of the same company. The proposed capital was to be £115,000 in shares with the usual borrowing powers and the first directors named in the Bill were: Lord Claud

Hamilton, Sir C. V. Blount, Bart., Sir G. R. Prescott, Bart., Mr. Lewis Hunt and Mr. J. G. Boucher. The estimated cost of the single track line was £144,481 10s 0d, which, at about £5,000 a mile, was considered a marvellously low figure. It was also proposed in the Bill that powers should be given to the company to enter into working agreements with the LBSCR, although it was expected that they would oppose the Bill at every stage.

The examination of the Bill by Messrs. Frere and Robinson, began on Monday, 27th January 1873, and every afternoon of that week was occupied by what Mr. Frere called 'this tedious contest'. There were numerous allegations of inaccuracies in the plans, many of which were sustained.[7] The examination went on into the following week until the Wednesday, when it was adjourned for engineers' and referees' reports.[8] The questions in conflict, which concerned the laying out of the line, the correctness of the levels and the accuracy of the deposited plans, were taken up again on the following Monday, and during the afternoon the examiner, Mr. Robinson, remarked:

'The opposition, as before stated, is ostensibly by the Brighton and South Eastern companies but what company or party, if any, is behind the promoters is not quite as clear; in any case it is evident that no effort has been spared to defeat the Bill in the early standing orders stage.'[9]

Quite suddenly it seems that the opposition withdrew its objections and shareholders of the LBSCR were informed by their chairman that this was in deference to local feelings at Eastbourne.[10] The Tunbridge Wells and Eastbourne Railway Company obtained its Act during 1873 and the scheme came under the wing of the South Eastern Railway.[11]

Some hard bargaining must have been going on during the following year, for early in 1875 Mr. Laing reported to the Brighton shareholders:

'. . . there was a small local line from Hailsham which we had no objection to and they got an Act a year ago. They have not been able, quite, to come to terms with us, they want rather more than we think they ought to have to work it as part of our line, and they have proposed a junction with the South Eastern. I think we may regard that as a matter of perfect indifference. I think we and the South Eastern understand one another and our own interests far too well to bid one against the other for any line of this description.'[12]

Mr. Laing had no doubt that a connection between Eastbourne and Tunbridge Wells would have to be effected but he told the meeting that they need have no fear of the SER. The Brighton directors must have been well aware, however, that the question was not as simple as that. Their company had a monopoly of the Eastbourne traffic and the SER wanted a share of that traffic. If the LBSCR and the TW & ER failed to come to some agreement the SER would have a share with very little effort.

Mr. Adams, a prominent shareholder of both the Brighton and the South Eastern companies, certainly had some doubts for he raised the question on the following day at the general meeting of the latter company. He asked the chairman, Sir Edward Watkin, to pledge that he would have nothing to do with connecting Eastbourne with Tunbridge Wells, for such unnecessary competition was costly to both companies. Sir Edward's reply was 'We have a truce with the Brighton company.'[13]

Only two weeks later, at a special General Meeting of the Tunbridge Wells and Eastbourne Railway Company, the chairman, Sir C. Blount, moved that they approve a Bill to authorise his company to construct their line to join up with the Tonbridge to Hastings branch of the SER. This was carried unanimously.[14]

The threat to the monopoly of the LBSCR at Eastbourne was becoming more urgent and must have prompted the company into more serious negotiations. In July 1875, when Mr. Laing was asked what had become of the Tunbridge Wells and Eastbourne Railway, he said that arrangements were being made with the local party and these would soon come up for confirmation by the shareholders.[15] At the same time Sir Edward Watkin, of the SER, was happy to announce the general principles of an agreement with Brighton for a share of the Eastbourne traffic.[16] At the end of the year it was reported that:

'The new direct line from Eastbourne to London, the extension of which we understand the directors of the LBSCR have pledged themselves to complete, it is intended shall run in a straight line from Eastbourne to Tunbridge Wells and join the main line of the SER at that station, passing next through Sevenoaks up to London.'[17]

Events began to move quite quickly for a while and in January 1876 the Brighton shareholders approved a Bill to vest in the LBSCR the undertakings of the TW & ER and to make better provision for railway communication to Eastbourne.[18] Sir Edward Watkin reported to the South Eastern shareholders that the outcome of the Eastbourne railway was a friendly agreement with the LBSCR, by which the Brighton company would build the line, the traffic would be shared, and the South Eastern would get about a quarter of the receipts.[19] In February the TW & ER shareholders approved a Bill to extend the period of their Act of 1873 and a Bill to vest their undertaking in the LBSCR.[20]

It will be remembered that the original Act of 1873 authorised the LBSCR to work the Eastbourne railway. For the Act of 1876 the acquiescence of the SER was necessary and this was purchased for £8,534, a share of the Eastbourne receipts, and running powers over the new line.[21] It was not until 1877 that Mr. Laing explained to the Brighton shareholders why their company had been saddled with the building of a railway line which was neither needed nor wanted. This was at a meeting convened in April to approve a Bill confirming the agreement with the SER. The Brighton company were bound to build the line, said Mr. Laing, otherwise it would have been taken to a point near Wadhurst on the South Eastern line and about half of the Eastbourne traffic would have been diverted. Under the agreement only a quarter of the receipts would be lost and the line would fill up that district and prevent any further competition.[22]

There were no further comments at that meeting, but when Parliamentary charges of about £10,000 appeared in the Half-Yearly Report in July, there were some questions at the General Meeting which followed. Mr. Adams referred at some length to 'charges that we are obliged to spend, one way and another, on a line we do not want.' In the opinion of Mr. Adams there was plenty of traffic for one line but not enough for two and he went on to complain of the attitude of the SER and of the powerful interests in the background which had forced events.

'It would be better for the South Eastern to develop their own territory than to encroach on ours. As I see it, we have been compelled to make an agreement with the South Eastern to divide the Eastbourne traffic. Nobody in that district would make a line except in the expectation of palming it off on one of the two great companies. The Duke of Devonshire, although a powerful man with an enormous income from that district, has no right to compel the small companies to spend unnecessarily.'[23]

Mr. Adams considered it neither patriotic nor proper of the Duke of Devonshire to do this in order to benefit his own property and in his opinion there could be no other object in view.

Mr. Laing repeated what he had said so often before, that the company did not want to make the line, and agreed that it was hard to see a place grow by their encouragement, only to have someone else profit from it at their expense. He then reminded the meeting that the Duke of Devonshire was a very wealthy and enterprising nobleman and if he chose to build a line from Eastbourne to somewhere on the Hastings line, the Brighton company would be unable to prevent it and at least half the Eastbourne traffic would be lost.

'The directors most reluctantly came to the conclusion that half a loaf was better than no bread and it was better to save two thirds or three fourths of the Eastbourne traffic than to lose half of it.'[24]

Referring to the parliamentary expenses, Mr. Laing said that it was always more expensive to take over a line than to construct one from the beginning. The new line caused more concern at the next General Meeting, when it was reported that there had been a falling off of pleasure travel to the south coast resorts. By this time the Surrey and Sussex Junction Railway was being revived and Mr. Adams wanted to know the total length of line, including 'that funny line to Eastbourne'.[25]

The year 1878 was a difficult one financially for the LBSCR and at the General Meeting, early in 1879, there was a great deal of hostility towards the new lines which were under construction. Mr. Adams again aired his views:

' . . . there is the Tunbridge Wells and Eastbourne Railway Act; that is an act you were forced into, but that is a country which can never pay. The South Eastern company, by pressing you, have got a portion of that traffic which they never ought to have got, and that £200,000 will never pay a ¼d, and not only will not pay, but the traffic will be divided.'

Mr. Laing reminded the meeting that 'if you get authority [to build a line] in good times, you cannot just drop it in bad.'[26]

The half-yearly accounts for the second half of 1879 showed that the sum of £8,000 had been paid to the SER as their share of the Eastbourne traffic.[27] At the General Meeting a few days later it was Mr. Adams who wanted to know what the SER had given in return for the £8,000. The line was not yet open, so no traffic could have been carried by that route. Mr. Laing explained that the agreement with the SER had a time limit, but the construction work on the line had proved difficult and the opening of the line was postponed. Under the agreement the payments were due from the beginning of the last half-year.

Mr. Laing went on to say:

'The South Eastern — to do them justice I must say it — did not promote that line. The proposal to make another line from Eastbourne to the South Eastern was got up by influential local parties with the Duke of Devonshire at their back . . . and we came to the conclusion that it was not safe to disregard it.'[28]

At the General Meeting of the South Eastern Railway, however, there was a note of triumph in Sir Edward Watkin's voice when he referred to the £8,000.

'Now gentlemen, there is a satisfactory feature of this account which I must call attention to, and that is . . . the receipts for the Eastbourne traffic.'[29]

Of course, the chairman of the SER was glad to be able to remark upon any satisfactory feature of the account, for the cut-throat competition with the LCDR was causing both of those companies serious financial difficulties.

Although not yet complete, there was an inspection of the line three weeks after these meetings and the official party included the following members: Mr. J. P. Knight, general manager of the LBSCR; Mr. P. Bannister, resident engineer of the LBSCR; Mr. A. H. Perry, district engineer; Mr. John Cripps, surveyor and estate agent; Mr. Goldsmith, assistant engineer; Mr. Firbank, the contractor (Joseph Firbank & Sons); Mr. Hodgson, representing Saxby & Farmer, signalling engineers; Mr. John Richardson, assistant superintendent; Mr. Houghton, telegraphic superintendent; Mr. Williams, traffic superintendent; and Mr. Ropes.

It is not clear how the party travelled but it left Eridge station at one o'clock on Friday, 13th February 1880, and made its way to Mayfield where lunch was taken under the presidency of Mr. Firbank. After lunch the party continued on to Hailsham where the new line joined the original branch from Polegate. The whole of the permanent way from Heathfield to Hailsham had been laid and was ready for use, with the exception of 100 yards and it was hoped that this section of the line would be open for traffic on 1st March.

Mr. Firbank expressed the opinion that he would be able to complete the remaining part of the line in about three months but the weather cannot have been very accommodating for Colonel Hutchinson was not able to inspect the southern section of the line until Saturday, 3rd April 1880, when he sanctioned its opening for passenger traffic. Three trains ran in each direction on that Saturday afternoon although the line was not formally opened for traffic until the following Monday. After the inspection Col. Hutchinson, accompanied by railway officials and Mr. Firbank, adjourned to the George Hotel at Hailsham.[30]

Referring to capital charges in the account presented at the half-yearly general meeting in July 1880, Mr. Laing again mentioned the necessity of spending money to prevent competing lines and to justify this he spoke of a South Eastern Railway proposal, some years earlier, to build a line from Maidstone to Ashford. This they had dropped because they did not want to spend the money and they now had a formidable competing line in a Bill now before the Lords. Mr. Laing again stressed that the twice yearly payment of £8,000 to the SER was better than losing £16,000 and in any case the losses had been more than recouped in the Portsmouth area where a new agreement had been negotiated with the London and South Western Railway, to the advantage of the Brighton company.[31]

The remainder of the line was opened to the public on 1st September 1880, but early in October it had to be closed again for a week. On the night of 9th October there was heavy rain in many parts of the country, including East Sussex, causing much damage and flooding. The first 'up' train on the Sunday morning of the 10th October was stopped short of Mayfield and sent back to Heathfield as the contractor's gangers had found two serious slips, one each side of Mayfield and at one point there was room under the track for a man to stand upright. It was the contractor's responsibility to maintain the track for the first year after the completion of the line and it was expected that normal services would be resumed on Monday, 18th October.[32]

There was still some disagreement at the end of 1882 as to the amount of the final account for settlement. On 21st January 1883 the Engineering Committee met to begin their inquiry into the accounts of Mr. Firbank for his contract for the Tunbridge Wells and Eastbourne line, which had been referred to the committee in the previous November. Mr. Bannister submitted his report and final account showing the following position:

Amount of Mr. Firbank's account as rendered:		£280,176 18 9
Deductions agreed to by Mr. Firbank:	£10,084 14 3	
Further deductions by Mr. Bannister but objected to by Mr. Firbank:	£31,160 5 8	£ 41,244 19 11
		£238,931 18 10
Less certificates paid:		£235,000 5 10
Balance:		£ 3,931 13 0
In addition to this Mr. Bannister recommends allowances to Mr. Firbank although not legally claimable by him:		£ 5,527 3 10
Amount recommended for payment as final settlement		£ 9,458 16 10

An early picture of Waldron showing a north-bound goods leaving the yard while a south-bound passenger is awaiting departure in the platform.

Horeham Road North Signal Box.

A letter from Mr. Firbank appealing to the Directors for their consideration of the deductions amounting to over £31,000 was read to the committee and after long discussion and Mr. Bannister having explained the nature of the deductions, the inquiry was adjourned until the next day. The inquiry was completed the next day and the secretary was instructed to write to Mr. Firbank and invite him to meet the committee on 30th January to which date the committee adjourned. After a long discussion on the subject of his accounts at the reconvened meeting, Mr. Firbank ultimately agreed to accept a payment from the company of £7,000 in settlement of all his claims in respect of the contract and he undertook at once to pay the company all outstanding charges for the carriage of materials amounting to £5,762 5s 8d. Unfortunately the reports and letters quoted in the committee minutes do not seem to have survived and it is not known if Mr. Firbank might have been nearly £2,500 better off if he had not met the committee.

References

1. Half-Yearly General Meeting, LBSCR. 22.7.1874.
2. Dendy-Marshall, C. F. *History of the Southern Railway.* Page 22.
3. 1856 — The Mayfield and Heathfield Railway. Engineer: Frederick Turner.
   1862 — The Tunbridge Wells and Eastbourne Railway. Engineer: Montague Harrison. Surveyor: J. W. Penfold. Depositor: William Elliott.
   1863 — The Tunbridge Wells and Eastbourne Railway. Engineers: George P. Bidder and Frederick D. Bannister (of the SER). Surveyors: Alexander and Littlewood.
4. *Herepath's Railway Journal.* 7.12.1872.
5. *East Sussex Journal.* 28.1.1873.
6. *Herepath's Railway Journal.* 1.2.1873.
7. *Herepath's Railway Journal.* 1.2.1873.
8. *Herepath's Railway Journal.* 8.2.1873.
9. *Herepath's Railway Journal.* 15.2.1873.
10. Half-Yearly General Meeting, LBSCR. 23.7.1873.
11. White, H. P. *A Regional History of the Railways of Great Britain, Vol. 2.* Page 93.
12. Half-Yearly General Meeting, LBSCR. 27.1.1875.
13. Half-Yearly General Meeting, SER. 28.1.1875.
14. *Herepath's Railway Journal.* 13.2.1875.
15. Half-Yearly General Meeting, LBSCR. 21.7.1875.
16. Half-Yearly General Meeting, SER. 29.7.1875.
17. *Herepath's Railway Journal.* 20.11.1875.
18. Half-Yearly General Meeting, LBSCR. 26.1.1876.
19. Half-Yearly General Meeting, SER. 27.1.1876.
20. *Herepath's Railway Journal.* 19.2.1876.
21. White, H. P. op. cit. page 93.
22. Special General Meeting, LBSCR. 21.4.1877.
23. Half-Yearly General Meeting, LBSCR. 25.7.1877.
24. 〃 〃 〃 〃 〃
25. *Herepath's Railway Journal.* 2.2.1878.
26. Half-Yearly General Meeting, LBSCR. 29.1.1879.
27. Half-Yearly Report. Jan. 1880.
28. Half-Yearly General Meeting, LBSCR. 21.1.1880.
29. Half-Yearly General Meeting, SER. 22.1.1880.
30. *Journal of the Brighton Circle Historical Society.* Vol. 6. No. 6. December, 1980. (M. J. Overbury).
31. Half-Yearly General Meeting, LBSCR. 21.7.1880.

POLEGATE, HEATHFIELD AND TUNBRIDGE WELLS LINE.

SINGLE LINE BETWEEN POLEGATE AND ERIDGE.—The Train Staff Stations are Polegate, Hailsham, Horeham Road, Heathfield, Mayfield, Rotherfield and Eridge.

WEEK DAYS.

m. c.	DOWN.	Short. Eng. A.M. dep.	Passngr. A.M. arr.	dep.	Short. A.M. arr.	dep.	Passngr. A.M. arr.	dep.	Short. P.M. arr.	dep.	Passngr. P.M. arr.	dep.
	Tunbridge Wells		7	7 24			10	10 7				1 46
3 7	Groombridge		7 26	7 27			10 13	10 14			1 52	1 53
5 7	Eridge	6 30 7 15	7 32	7 33			10 19	10 20			1 58	1 59
8 18	Rotherfield		7 45	7 46			10 32	10 33			2 11	2 12
10 79	Mayfield		7 54	7 55			10 41	10 42			2 20	2 21
14 55	Heathfield		8 8	8 9			10 55	10 56			2 34	2 35
17 1	Horeham Road		8 15	8 16			11 5	11 6			2 41	2 42
20 65	Hellingly		8 25	8 26		8 50	11 12	11 13			2 51	2 52
22 29	Hailsham	6 38 7 22	8 31	8 33	8 58		11 18	11 20		12 17	1 45 2 57	2 59
25 27	Polegate		8 41		10 8		11 28		1 25		3 7	

WEEK DAYS—continued.

m. c.	DOWN.	B Goods. P.M. arr.	dep.	Short. P.M. arr.	dep.	Passngr. P.M. arr.	dep.	Short. P.M. arr.	dep.	Passngr. P.M. arr.	dep.
	Tunbridge Wells					3 18					9 25
3 7	Groombridge	2 50	3 0 3 10			3 24	3 25			9 31	9 32
5 7	Eridge	3 20 3 45				3 30	3 31			9 37	9 38
8 18	Rotherfield	4 5 4 20				3 43	3 44			9 50	9 51
10 79	Mayfield	4 45 5 0				3 52	3 53			9 59	10 0
14 55	Heathfield	5 20 5 45				4 6	4 7		6 2	10 13	10 14
17 1	Horeham Road	5 57 6 10				4 13	4 14		6 9	10 20	10 21
20 65	Hellingly	6 25 6 26				4 23	4 24		6 15	10 30	10 31
22 29	Hailsham	6 35 7 25		5 30	6 40	4 29	4 31	6 48	6 28	9 25 10 36	
25 27	Polegate	7 40 8 15		5 38	4 18	4 39			6 37 7 13 7 15		

SUNDAYS.

m. c.	DOWN.	Passngr. A.M. arr.	dep.	Short. A.M. arr.	dep.	Passngr. A.M. arr.	dep.	Short. P.M. arr.	dep.	Passngr. P.M. arr.	dep.
	Tunbridge Wells		6 17				10 28				9 40
3 7	Groombridge	6 23	6 24			10 34	10 35			9 46	9 47
5 7	Eridge	6 29	6 30			10 40	10 41			9 52	9 53
8 18	Rotherfield	6 42	6 43			10 53	10 54			10 5	10 6
10 79	Mayfield	6 51 6 53				11 2 11 3				10 14 10 15	
14 55	Heathfield	7 6 7 7				11 16 11 17		7 12		10 28 10 29	
17 1	Horeham Road	7 13 7 14				11 23 11 24		7 32 7 33		10 35 10 36	
20 65	Hellingly	7 23 7 24		2 0		11 33 11 34		7 43		10 45 10 46	
22 29	Hailsham	7 29 7 31		2 8		9 20 11 39 11 41		8 50 7 48 7 50		8 50 10 51	
25 27	Polegate	7 59				11 49				11 1	

B Runs to Eastbourne, and is due there at 8.25 p.m.

Extract from working timetable for September 1880.

POLEGATE, HEATHFIELD AND TUNBRIDGE WELLS LINE.

SINGLE LINE BETWEEN POLEGATE AND ERIDGE.—The Train Staff Stations are Polegate, Hailsham, Horeham Road, Heathfield, Mayfield, Rotherfield and Eridge.

WEEK DAYS.

m. c.	UP.	Passngr. A.M. arr.	dep.	Short. A.M. arr.	dep.	Passngr. A.M. arr.	dep.	Short. A.M. H arr.	dep.	Goods. A.M. arr.	dep.	D Goods. A.M. arr.	dep.	Passngr. A.M. arr.	dep.	Short. H arr.	dep.	Passngr. P.M. arr.	dep.	Short. P.M. arr.	dep.
	Polegate				6 50				9 10		7 10		7 50 9 30			9 18			12 43		1 0
78	Hailsham	6 26		6 58		6 31		7 52		9 18	7 54 8 0		9 45 10 10		5 10		12 51 12 52		12 53		1 8
62	Hellingly	6 32				7 52		7 59 8 0			10 12		10 29		5 10		12 58		1 13		
29	Horeham Road	6 46				8 14 8 15		8 25			10 28		10 44 10 45		5 13		1 13 1 14				
72	Heathfield	6 57				8 42		8 50			11 25		11 55 11 56		5 12		1 24 1 25				
28	Mayfield	7 13				8 51		9 0			12 35		11 11 11 12		5 12		1 40 1 41				
9	Rotherfield	7 22 7 23				8 59 9 0		9 6			1 5		11 29 11 30		5 17		1 49 1 50				
20	Eridge	7 31 7 32				9 9		9 13			1 25 1 40		11 35 11 36		1 30		1 58 1 59			9 45	
20	Groombridge	7 37 7 38									1 50		11 43				2 4 2 5				
27	Tunbridge Wells	7 45				9 13					1 60						2 12			9 53	

WEEK DAYS—continued.

m. c.	UP.	Short. P.M. arr.	dep.	Passngr. P.M. arr.	dep.	Short. P.M. arr.	dep.	Goods. P.M. arr.	dep.	Passngr. P.M. arr.	dep.	Short. P.M. arr.	dep.
	Polegate	2 50		4 55		6 3		5 55		7 5	7 15		
78	Hailsham	2 58		5 3 5 6			6 3		7 13 7 20		7 15 7 20		8 13
62	Hellingly			5 11					7 36		7 36		
29	Horeham Road			5 25 5 26					7 46 7 47		7 46 7 47		
72	Heathfield			5 36 5 37					8 3		8 11 8 3		
28	Mayfield			5 52 5 53					8 12		8 20 8 12		
9	Rotherfield			6 1 6 2					8 21		8 26 8 21		
20	Eridge			6 10 6 11					8 27		8 34 8 27		
20	Groombridge			6 16 6 17									
27	Tunbridge Wells			6 24									

D Starts from Eastbourne 7.30 a.m.   H These are mixed Passenger and Goods Train.

SUNDAYS.

m. c.	UP.	Short. P.M. arr.	dep.	Passngr. P.M. arr.	dep.	Passngr. A.M. arr.	dep.	Short. P.M. arr.	dep.	Passngr. P.M. arr.	dep.	Short. P.M. arr.	dep.
	Polegate	2 58			5			8 35		4 26		9 17	
78	Hailsham			6 5 6 11		6 10		3 43		4 34 4 36		9 25 9 27	
62	Hellingly			6 26		6 10				4 41 4 42		9 32 9 33	
29	Horeham Road			6 37		6 25 6 36 6 37				4 56 4 57		9 47 9 48	
72	Heathfield			6 52 6 53		6 52 6 53				5 7 5 8		9 58 9 59	
28	Mayfield			7 1 7 2		7 6 7 7				5 24		10 14 10 15	
9	Rotherfield			7 10 7 11		7 13 7 14				5 32 5 33		10 23 10 24	
20	Eridge			7 16 7 17		7 23 7 24				5 41 5 42		10 32 10 33	
20	Groombridge					7 29 7 31				5 47 5 48		10 38 10 39	
27	Tunbridge Wells			7 24		7 59				5 55		10 46	

CHAPTER THREE

OPERATION

I
T is not really possible to consider the passenger services on the Tunbridge Wells to Eastbourne line in isolation from the rest of the railway system in East Sussex. The services fell into the pattern of traffic for the whole area and trains connected with London services at Groombridge or Eridge, at the northern end of the line, and at Polegate in the south. The pattern was first established during the late 1860s when the branch lines were being extended. In 1865 there were nine passenger trains in each direction, on weekdays, between Three Bridges and East Grinstead and six trains in each direction between Lewes and Uckfield.[1] Both of these branches were worked by self-contained shuttle services and when the branches were extended to Tunbridge Wells in 1866 and 1868 the existing services were projected on to the new terminus. Over the next twenty years the railway network became more complex but the level of the services was not increased to any great extent.

Using some of the earthworks of the abandoned Surrey and Sussex Junction Railway, the line from Croydon to East Grinstead via Oxted was completed and opened in 1884 but in the following year there were still only twelve trains from London, on weekdays, as far as Oxted. Three of these belonged to the SER and they continued on to Tonbridge via the Crowhurst spur. Of the other nine Brighton trains four terminated at Oxted and five went on to East Grinstead and beyond. At the same time there were six weekday trains in each direction running between Three Bridges and Tunbridge Wells and these shared the section of line from Groombridge to Tunbridge Wells with seven trains from Lewes and five or more trains from Eastbourne making this the most intensively occupied section, even in those early days.[2] Oxted and Groombridge were connected in 1888 allowing a more direct service between London and Tunbridge Wells which also had to merge with existing services at Groombridge.

During the last decade of the nineteenth century and the early part of this century considerable building development took place in the Sanderstead and Oxted areas and the towns of East Grinstead, Uckfield and Tunbridge Wells were growing rapidly. Passenger traffic showed a steady increase and season ticket holders were forming a significant proportion of the traffic north of East Grinstead.[3] Single track was no longer sufficient for the Uckfield line and this was doubled in 1894. For the last one and a quarter miles into Eridge this line had run parallel with the single track from Eastbourne and when it was doubled the Uckfield line became the up road and the Eastbourne line the down road, with a new junction and signal box at Redgate Mill.

By 1904 the services had assumed a pattern which was to persist with very little alteration, even after 1933 when the electrification of the main line from London to Brighton, completed in 1931, made its full impact. Basically the service was operated between London and Brighton or Tunbridge Wells via East Grinstead, and between London and Tunbridge Wells via Edenbridge with connec-

tions or through coaches for the Uckfield line to Brighton or the Heathfield line to Eastbourne. Trains to Tunbridge Wells from Brighton or Eastbourne connected with the London services at Groombridge resulting in a very busy interchange of traffic at what would normally have been a quiet country station serving a small village. With eight daily trains in each direction on the Eastbourne line added to those using the Brighton, Three Bridges and London lines, there was a total of eighty-three workings through Groombridge each day during the summer of 1904.[4] By 1912 this figure had increased to one hundred and fifteen.[5]

Although the single track spur from Ashurst to Birchden was completed in 1880 it was not used, except as a locomotive graveyard, because it would seem that there was little point, at this time, in trains avoiding Tunbridge Wells.[6] Even when the Oxted to Groombridge line was opened in 1888, trains which included through carriages from London for Brighton or Eastbourne detached them at Groombridge for transfer to the connecting services out of Tunbridge Wells.[7] Growing season ticket sales from Crowborough, however, led to the need for direct train services with London and the Ashurst to Birchden spur was doubled and brought into use on 7th June 1914. From this date the trains which used the new route between London and the two coastal towns, used Eridge station for the transfer of through carriages if they were included. Connecting services were also provided at Eridge for those passengers who wished to use these trains between London and Tunbridge Wells and this is discussed more fully in Chapter 12.[8]

The short single track spur between the two stations at Tunbridge Wells was built by the LBSCR but worked by the South Eastern Railway who were taking advantage of the running powers granted under the agreement of 1876. The only use which that company made of the connection, however, was for four round trips a day between Tonbridge and the LBSCR station at Tunbridge Wells, apart from a short period in 1884 and 1885 when two through trains from Charing Cross to Eastbourne and return used the route. The SER preferred to draw their share of the Eastbourne receipts without any further effort or expense. After the formation of the Southern Railway in 1923, however, many of the services from Brighton and some of those from Eastbourne were extended to Tonbridge and even beyond. By the early 1930s one of the trains from Eastbourne continued on to Guildford via Tonbridge and Redhill and one of the trains to Eastbourne originated at Redhill,[9] a practice which continued into the British Railways period. By the end of the 1920s there were also daily services between the Medway towns and the south coast via Maidstone, Paddock Wood, Tonbridge and Tunbridge Wells.

In order to consider the services of the Tunbridge Wells to Eastbourne line in greater detail extracts have been taken from the timetables of several distinct periods in the history of the line and these are shown in graphic form. When, in 1880, the first part of the line opened as far as Heathfield, six trains in each direction provided the services and one of those in the up direction was classified as a mixed train. There was no reference to goods traffic in the down direction in that first timetable. The full opening of the line on 1st September 1880, saw the introduction of the daily through goods train which was scheduled to depart from Eastbourne at 7.50 a.m. and it was due at Tunbridge Wells exactly six hours later. The return working left Tunbridge Wells at 2.50 p.m. and this was due back at Polegate at 8.15 p.m. The passenger service consisted of six trains in each direction but this was reduced to five in the following year. Loads were to be restricted to eight to ten vehicles according to the weather conditions and the locomotive available, one bogie vehicle counting as two vehicles.

Apart from slight variations in timings the same time-table applied until 1884 when the SER introduced their through services which were timed as follows:

DOWN			
Charing Cross	depart	11.20 a.m.	5.35 p.m.
Tunbridge Wells	arrive	12.15 p.m.	6.35 p.m.
,, ,,	depart	12.17 p.m.	6.37 p.m.
Eastbourne	arrive	1.24 p.m.	7.44 p.m.

UP			
Eastbourne	depart	9.30 a.m.	3.15 p.m.
Tunbridge Wells	arrive	10.38 a.m.	4.13 p.m.
,, ,,	depart	10.39 a.m.	4.14 p.m.
Charing Cross	arrive	11.35 a.m.	5.05 p.m.

The same timings applied during 1885 until the service was withdrawn at the end of the year. The afternoon down train was stabled overnight at Eastbourne and formed the up train the following morning. Being non-stop between Eastbourne and Tunbridge Wells, the journey time between the two towns was only just over the hour. The trains included a Hastings portion between Tonbridge and Charing Cross.[10]

Other timetable developments came towards the end of 1894. A daily goods service from Polegate to Heath-field and return was introduced and the provision of improved motive power enabled the through goods timings to be improved. Traffic had increased during the first few years of the line and the ageing 'Craven' loco-motives found it increasingly difficult to cope with the volume. It was not unusual for wagons to be left behind especially when fallen leaves or bad weather caused the rails to become slippery. Additional power was required and the choice was between designing a new locomotive and modifying an existing one. The latter course was chosen since only one was required and Mr. Stroudley successfully fitted a larger boiler and cylinders to the class E1 0—6—0 tank engine No. 157 *Barcelona* which was then designated class E Special. Apart from the occasions when it was in the works for general repairs *Barcelona* worked the daily goods in the up direction from 1884 until 1921. The return working was at the head of a passenger train. During 1896 a class E3 0—6—2 tank No. 170 was transferred to Eastbourne to replace No. 157 while it was in for repairs. On the return of No. 157 from the works No. 170 was transferred to Tunbridge Wells to work the daily goods in the down direction and as late as 1928 No. 170 and another of the class, No. 457,

were still regularly working the line. The improved goods services were timed as follows:[11]

UP			
Polegate	depart	7.02 a.m.	9.00 a.m.
Heathfield	arrive	7.56 a.m.	
Tunbridge Wells	arrive		1.35 p.m.

DOWN			
Tunbridge Wells	depart		2.30 p.m.
Heathfield	depart	8.50 a.m.	
Polegate	arrive	11.50 a.m.	7.05 p.m.

1884 also saw the beginnings of the poultry traffic. A ten ton vacuum brake fitted van, No. 8014, was equipped with shelves and kept for the conveyance of poultry only, from Heathfield to London, on Mondays, Wednesdays and Fridays, returning empty on Tuesdays, Thursdays and Saturdays. In October 1891 a second van, No. 3683, was provided and this worked from Heathfield on Tuesdays and Thursdays and returned empty on the following days. A third van, No. 8025, was provided in November 1900, and from this date until at least 1921 vans 3683 and 8025 were used on Mondays, Wednesdays and Fridays and No. 8014 was used on Tuesdays and Thursdays. During 1912 they were attached to the passenger train leaving Heathfield at 8.20 p.m. for Pole-gate where they were attached to a London bound goods train from Eastbourne. The empty vans were returned by goods train to Groombridge where they were attached to the first available passenger train from Tunbridge Wells to Heathfield. A similar routine was worked by van No. 8033 from Uckfield.

With a few variations the basic timetable remained much the same from 1886 until the end of the century although by this time the passenger services had been increased. During 1890 the Heathfield goods was extended to Eridge on Hailsham cattle market days, which were held once a month, and during 1900 it was extended to Rotherfield, except on Hailsham cattle market days. Also in 1900 came the introduction of two daily goods trains to Hellingly and presumably these brought materials for the building of the East Sussex Asylum. Hellingly continued to have a daily goods service well into British Railways days although the service was conditional upon requirements after the Second World War. With the completion of the building of the asylum in 1903, a passenger service to Hellingly was introduced in October of that year and as Hellingly was an intermediate station in a section of single line, all the trains on these services were required to return the token to Hailsham as they had not proceeded through the section.

By 1912 there were eight weekday passenger trains in each direction which travelled the whole length of the line, taking on average an hour and a half for the journey of almost thirty miles. This may seem a leisurely pace but the line had been built as cheaply as possible with many sharp curves and steep gradients. In addition to the eight through trains, a shuttle service was provided between Eastbourne and Hailsham, the number of trains varying according to the day of the week. There was also one train each morning from Eastbourne to Hellingly which returned to Polegate, and on Saturdays and alternate Wednesdays from June 12th to September 18th inclusive,

Eastbourne as depicted on an Edwardian postcard.

Cty. R. C. Riley

one of the afternoon Hailsham trains was extended to Hellingly for the benefit of visitors to the asylum. Heathfield, the only place of any size between Hailsham and Tunbridge Wells, also served as the terminus for two trains from Eastbourne and one from Tunbridge Wells. The second of the Eastbourne trains waited at Heathfield for one hour and fourteen minutes before returning to Eastbourne with the poultry vans attached. The train from Tunbridge Wells waited almost an hour before making its return journey and there was a period of twenty minutes during which both trains were at Heathfield while one of the through trains paused on its way to Eastbourne.

Although the line was single between Hailsham and Redgate Mill Junction trains travelling in opposite directions were able to cross at each of the stations on the line except Hellingly. Some trains would have to wait several minutes for the train from the opposite direction, which would account for the differences in times taken to complete the journey.

At this time thirty trains a day left London for Tunbridge Wells and eight of these provided the connecting services at Groombridge for Eastbourne line trains. At the other end of the line, at Polegate, it was also possible to get a connection to London using the main line via Lewes and there were eleven connecting services at this station. In the opposite direction sixteen services from London connected with trains for Hailsham and the Tunbridge Wells line at Polegate and the eight through trains all met with connecting London services at Groombridge. The passenger for London from Eastbourne or Polegate, therefore, had the choice of two routes and as the fares were the same the question of time would probably be the deciding factor. The new 'direct' route to London took up to an hour longer than the old one and even the passenger from Hailsham would gain half an hour by using the Lewes route. In his case, however, the quicker route would also be slightly more expensive as the mileage was greater. In addition to the connecting services with London, through carriages were included in the 11.10 a.m. down train from Victoria to Tunbridge Wells and the 7.55 a.m. and 9.55 a.m. up trains from Eastbourne to Tunbridge Wells. These carriages were detached and attached to their connecting trains at Groombridge. For the convenience of passengers who wished to have their own private transport at the end of their journey, certain trains were permitted to convey carriage trucks and horse-boxes and these vehicles were kept at a number of stations. The railway company advised users of this service to give at least one day's notice at the station where they were required in order to avoid disappointment. Open and covered carriage

EASTBOURNE, POLEGATE, ERIDGE AND TUNBRIDGE WELLS LINE.

SINGLE LINE BETWEEN POLEGATE & REDGATE MILL JUNC., Worked under Electric Train Staff Regulations.—The Train Staff Stations are Polegate, Hailsham, Waldron, Heathfield, Mayfield, Rotherfield & Mark Cross, & Redgate Mill Junc.

Time must not be made up in running down inclines.

M. c.	DOWN WEEK-DAYS.	Pass. A.M.	Pass. A.M.	Goods A.M.	Passngr. A.M.	Passngr. A.M. A	Pass A.M.	Goods A.M.	Passngr. A.M.	Goods. A.M.	P'ssng'r P.M. A	Pas P.M.	Pass. P.M.	Pas P.M.
	Tunbridge Wells, L. B. & S. C.	dep	arr. dep.	arr. dep.	arr dep.	arr. dep. A	dep.	arr. dep.	arr. dep.	arr. dep.	dep.	dep	arr. dep	dep
		... 7 8			... 9 5		... 1055			... 1215		... 150	
3 3	Groombridge ..	... 714 718			... 9 11 9 14		... 1016 1019		1221 1224		156 159	
5 3	Eridge	... 722 723			9 18 9 23		11 1 11 5		1228 1229		2 3 2 4	
6 23	Redgate Mill J.	... 725 726			9 25 9 26		11 9 1110		1231 1232		2 7 2 8	
8 13	Rotherfield * ..	... 730 731			9 30 9 31		1113 1114		11 1 1236 1237		212 214	
10 72	Mayfield	739 740			9 39 9 40		1127 1128		1245 1246		222 223	
14 54	Heathfield	751 752			9 51 9 53		1110 1111		1257 1258		234 235	
17 15	Waldron ‡	8 0 8 1			10 1 10 2	1134 1135	1148 1149	1 35 1 45	1 6 1 13		243 244	
20 63	Hellingly	8 9 8 11		9 36	1010 1011	1119	1143 1157 1158	1 52 2 23	1 21 1 22		251 252	
22 45	Hailsham	625 815 825	9 39 9 40	10 0	1015 1017	1124 1147 1148	12 2 12 3	2 29 2 37	1 26 1 27	140 256 258 330	
25 41	Polegate	633 832 834	949 1015	10 7 1012	1024 1016	1131 1245 1210 1213	245 4 51	3 4 1 36	150 3 5 11 338	
27 59	Hampden Park	651 838 39	1020	1016 1031 1032		4 10	1 40 165 315 316	
29 58	Eastbourne ..	655 844	1020	1036	1255	1220	4 15	1 43	2 0 320	

	DOWN WEEK-DAYS—contd.	Pass. P.M.	Goods. P.M.	Pas P.M.	Passenger P.M. A	Gs. P.M.	Pasngr P.M.	Pas P.M.	Pass. P.M.	Pass P.M.	Passngr. P.M.	Passngr. P.M.	Passngr. P.M.
		arr dep	arr. dep.	arr dep.	arr dep.	dep.	arr dep.	dep.	arr dep.	dep	arr. dep.	dep.	arr. dep.
	T. Wells, L.B.&S.C		... 4 25	... 4 43	... 555	... 640				... 9 35
	Groombridge..........		4 31 4 34	4 49 4 50	6 1 6 3	646 650			Thursdays only, and in June only.	Weds. & Sats. excepted July. Commencing July.	Wednesdays and Saturdays only.	9 43 9 46 47
	Eridge		440 4 54	4 54 4 58	6 6 6 7	654 655				9 479 48
	Redgate Mill Junc		5 6 5 9	5 1 5 2	6 10 611	657 658				9 519 52
	Rotherfield *		515 5 29	5 6 5 8	615 616	7 2 7 3				9 569 57
	Mayfield	... 335	537 5 55	5 16 5 18	624 625	711 712				10 510
	Heathfield		6 76 25	530 532	636	723 724	820			1019 1020
	Waldron ‡	343 344	635 7 0	5 40 5 41		732 733 828 829			1027 1028
	Hellingly	352 353	B	5 49 5 50		741 742 837 838			1035 1036
	Hailsham	357 4 0	435 716 7 25 525 5 26	6 4 5 55 620		665 746 750 842 843		9 45	9 45	1040 1041
	Polegate	4 7	442 5 735 735 536 6 2 6 5	630	7 3 757 852 855 9 52 10 3	0 52 10 3	1048 1049
	Hampden Park	510 511	8a 0 541 6 9 10		7 48 8 59 9 0 7 10 8 10 7 10 8	10 3	1053
	Eastbourne	516	9a 0 545 6 14	810 9 5	1013	1013	1057

	DOWN WEEK-DAYS—contd.	Eng F.M.	Eng. A.M.	Ety. P.M.	Empty P.M.		Passngr. A.M.	Mtr. A.M.	Passngr. A.M.	Pas P.M.	Passngr. P.M.	Mtr. P.M.	Pas P.M.	Passngr. P.M.
		dep.	dep.	dep. C	arr.		arr dep.	dep.	arr. dep.	dep.	arr. dep.	dep.	arr dep.	arr. dep.
	T. Wells, L.B.&S.C						... dep	8 10	... 102			6 10		... 5 27
	High Rocks Halt...						8 19			6 14	
	Groombridge						8 23	1026 1030	4 14 4 18	6 18	3 33 9 43
	Eridge						8 28	10 2 1033	4 22 4 23 6 23	3 41 8 42
	Redgate Mill Junc			Thursdays and Mondays, Tuesdays and Saturdays in June, July, August and in September on Fridays also.	Weds. & Frids. only in June, July and August and only in September.	Thursdays only.	SUNDAYS.	8 31	1036 1037	4 26 4 27 6 30	3 45 8 45
	Rotherfield *						8 36	1041 1042	4 31 4 32 6 31	3 50 8 51
	Mayfield						8 45	1050 1051	4 40 4 26 6 40	3 59 9 0
	Heathfield						9 56	11 2 11 4	4 53 4 56 6 50	4 11 9 12
	Waldron ‡						9 4	1112 1113	5 4 5	4 20 9 21
	Hellingly				1052		9 12	1121 1122	5 13 5 14	4 28 9 28
	Hailsham		1050	11 5	1147		7 15 9 17 9 36 1127 1130 2 255 19 5 21 7 45 8 37 4 34 9 35
	Polegate	1050	1058	1113 1154 1155	9 50 1140 1142 2 355 28 5 35 7 51 8 45 4 39 9 44
	Hampden Park	1057		12 0	7 4 7 48 150 3 9 40 8 0 8 51 4 5 9 48
	Eastbourne		11 7 1120 12 5	7 52 10 0 1150 2 45 4 5 8 50 9 52

B On Saturdays, also on alternate Wednesdays, June 12th and 26th, July 10th and 24th, August 7th and 21st; September 4th and 18th, starts from Hellingly at 4.32 p.m., calls at Hailsham 4.36, 4.37 p.m. and arrives Polegate 4.44 p.m. C Empty Train shunted at Hailsham, and Engine run on Light to Eastbourne as shown. * Rotherfield and Mark Cross. ‡ Waldron and Horeham Rd.

Time must not be made up in running down inclines.

M. c.	UP WEEK-DAYS.	Goods. A.M.	Gds. A.M.	Goods A.M.	Passngr. A.M. A	Passngr. A.M. A	Passnger A.M.	Passngr A.M. .w	Goods A.M. A B	Goods. A.M. N	Pass. A.M.
		arr. dep	A.M.	arr. dep.	arr. dep.	arr. dep.	arr. dep.	arr. dep.	arr. dep.	arr. dep.	dep.
	Eastbourne	... 5 0		... 6a40	... 6 45	... 7 55	... 850	... 9 55	...	... 1018	... 1040
1 79	Hampden Park ...	... 5 5		6a45 6 49 6 50	...	8 54 855 9 59 10 0		... 1023	
4 17	Polegate	510 850 5 55 6a50 7 17 6 54 6 57	8 3 8 7 8 59 9 7	10 5 10 9	... 1030	1027 1133 1049 11 2 1230
7 13	Hailsham	9 09 10 6 5 7 27 7 28 7 47 5 815 817 9 14	1016 1017 1040 1041	1143 12 5 11 9 1110 1237
7 75	Hellingly	9 15 ... 7 33 7 97 10 8 22 8 24	1021 1022 1046	1211 1114 ...
12 43	Waldron ‡	... 745 812 7 187 19 8 32 8 34	1030 1031 1056 1057	1222 1233 ...
14 5	Heathfield	825 9 5 7 27 7 28 8 42 8 43	1039 1040 1110	1245 1 5 ...
18 66	Mayfield	917 950 739 744 8 54 8 56	1051 1052	1 17 1 47 ...
21 31	Rotherfield*	7 5 7 6	7 527 549 9 3 9 6	11 0 11 1	1 57 2 25 ...
23 35	Redgate Mill Junc.	... 10 0 7 59 8 0 9 8 9 9	11 9 1112	2 30 2 32 ...
24 66	Eridge	8 3 8 4 9 12 9 13	11 9 1112 When necessary.	2 35 2 58 ...
26 55	Groombridge	8 8 8 10 9 18 9 20	1116 1118	3 5 3 37 ...
29 53	T. Wells L. B. & S.C	8 16 9 26	1124	3 47

	UP WEEK-DAYS—contd.	Passngr. P.M. J K	Pasngr. P.M.	Passngr. P.M.	Pasngr. P.M. A	Ps P.M.	Passngr. P.M.	Passng P.M.	Pas P.M.	Passngr P.M.	Passngr. P.M.	Pasngr P.M.	Pass. P.M.
		arr. dep	arr. dep	... dep.	arr. dep	...	arr. ...	arr. ...	dp	... dp	... dep.	arr. dep	arr dep
	Eastbourne	... 1240	... 235	... 2 50	... 340		... 442	... ...	... 550	... 625		... 730	... 915	915 ...
	Hampden Park ...	1244 1245 239 240 2 51 2 55 344 345	... 446 447	... 555 629 630	... 734	919 919 ...
	Polegate	1249 1251 244 250 2 59 3 10 343 351 415 452 455 5 5 3 634 635	610 642 643	738 739 924 925 924 925 ...
	Hailsham	1258 1259 257 3 23 17 358 359 42 5 3 5 12	647 648	746 747 932 932 ...
	Hellingly	... 3 6 3 7 4 12 413 D 5 7 5 9	656 658	8 0 8 1 ...
	Waldron ‡	1 12 1 15 315 316 4 21 4 22 517 519	7 6	8 8 8 9 ...
	Heathfield	1 23 1 24 324 4 28 4 29 526 534	723 8 8 ...
	Mayfield	1 35 1 36 433 434 543 547	736 737 820 821 ...
	Rotherfield*	1 44 1 45 441 442 555 556	745 746 829 830 ...
	Redgate Mill Junc.	1 49 1 50 446 447 6 0 6 1	750 751 834 835 ...
	Eridge	1 53 1 54 450 452 6 4 6 6	754 755 838 839 ...
	Groombridge	1 58 2 0 456 458 610 613	759 8 1 843 845 ...
	T. Wells L.&S.O	2 5 5 0 619	8 7 851 ...

	UP WEEK-DAYS contd.	Pass. P.M.	Pass. P.M.	Pass. P.M.	Pass. P.M.	Pas P.M.	Mtr P.M.	Passngr. P.M.	Pas P.M.	Pass. P.M.	Mtr. P.M.	Pas P.M.
		arr. dep.	arr. dep.	arr. dep.		arr. dep.	dep.	arr. dep.	dep.	arr. dep.	dep.	dep.
	Eastbourne	... 9 15	... 10 20	... 11 20		... 7 189 0	... 1020	...	... 5 45	... 10	3 15 30
	Hampden Park ...	9 19 10 24 10 25 11 24 11 25	2 227 239 6	1024 1025	5 14 6 15	3 20
	Polegate	9 24 9 25 10 29 10 30 11 31 11 30 11 32	2 77 31 7 9 11 925	1029 1030 5 11 5 54 6 19 21	5 25 10 0
	Hailsham	9 32 9 33 10 38 10b43 11d40	2 77 38 7 39 9 18	1037 1039 3 14 25 28 6 30	5 32 10 7
	Hellingly	9 37 9 38 10b47	2 77 43 7 45 930	1042 1043	5 34 5 36
	Waldron ‡	9 46 9 47	7 53 7 55 938	1051 1052	5 44 5 46
	Heathfield	9 55 9 56	2 8 3 945 11 0 11 3	5 51 6 56 7 40
	Mayfield	10 6 1011	4 11 4 11 956 114 1111	7 7 7 57 51
	Rotherfield*	1018 1019	4 23 8 24 10 4 123 1124	7 17 7 19 7 59
	Redgate Mill J.	1023 1024	4 28 8 29 10 8 128 1129	7 23 7 24 3 0
	Eridge	1027 1028	4 32 3 33 1013 132 1133	7 27 7 28 8 6
	Groombridge	1032 1034	4 37 8 39 1017 137 1139	7 32 7 34 8 12
	High Rocks H.		d 4 45	7 40 8 19
	Tunbridge W.	1040	J 1022 145	8 19

* Rotherfield and Mark Cross. ‡ Waldron and Horeham Road. J On Hailsham Cattle Market Days, Live Stock 1. Horse Boxes or Cattle Vans (properly titted) may be attached at Hailsham to this Train, the Engine of the 12.50 p.m. short Train from Polegate being used to do the necessary shunting at Hailsham. K An extra Third Class Carriage to be run in this Train on alternate Wednesdays. D On Saturdays, also on alternate Wednesdays, June 12th and 26th, July 10th and 24th, August 7th and 21st, September 4th and 18th, runs on to Hellingly, due arrive at 4.27 p.m. a Engine only.

Extract from 1912 Service Timetable

Tunbridge Wells station around the turn of the century. *Lens of Sutton*

trucks were available, the latter costing five shillings for up to fifty miles and ten shillings for longer journeys, above the normal charge. A groom travelling with a horse was charged according to his class of travel but if he travelled in the horse-box the third class fare was charged.

The Sunday service was a very much reduced one with only one morning, one afternoon and one evening train in each direction, all with London connections. In addition a motor train made a trip from Tunbridge Wells to Hailsham and return in the morning and a trip from Tunbridge Wells to Heathfield and return in the evening. Special fares were normally charged for travel by these trains but this does not seem to have applied to the 'Sundays Only' service on the Tunbridge Wells line. The motor trains were officially regarded as additional to the ordinary service and the company reserved the right to withdraw them without previous notice.

No goods train worked on Sundays at any time in the history of the line and as far back as 1891 special arrangements were made for the Sunday milk traffic. A large quantity of milk came from Mayfield and through vans ran from this station to London Bridge and Victoria. On Sundays these were attached to the 7.18 a.m. passenger train from Eastbourne and transferred at Groombridge to the passenger train leaving Tunbridge Wells for Victoria at 8.32 a.m. At East Croydon those vans for London Bridge were transferred to a milk train which left there at 10.45 a.m. The empty vans left London Bridge with the 1.33 p.m. milk train for East Croydon where they were attached to the 2.30 p.m. passenger train from Victoria and transferred again at Groombridge to the Eastbourne line passenger train leaving Tunbridge Wells at 4.08 p.m.

The goods traffic seems to have reached its peak at this period and there is no doubt that the existence of the railway contributed enormously to the development of the area. In 1912 the first goods train of the day left Eastbourne at 5.00 a.m. and drew into the yard at Polegate ten minutes later. For two hours and forty minutes the

engine carried out shunting duties before continuing on to Hailsham at 8.30 a.m. Ten minutes were allowed at Hailsham for setting down and picking up wagons after which the train went on to Hellingly. Twenty minutes were allowed here and at 9.25 a.m. the train returned to Polegate where the engine carried out further shunting duties before terminating at Hampden Park at 10.20 a.m.

While the above train was carrying out its first spell of shunting duty at Polegate a light engine left Eastbourne at 6.40 a.m. to pick up a goods train at Polegate for Rotherfield. Nearly half an hour was spent at Polegate before the train continued with wagons for all stations to Rotherfield except Hailsham and Hellingly. At least twenty minutes were allowed at Waldron, Heathfield and Mayfield and an hour was allowed at Rotherfield for the train to turn round and return to Heathfield where it arrived at 11.22 a.m. In the meantime, when it was considered necessary, a third goods train left Polegate at 10.30 a.m. for Heathfield where it arrived at 11.10 a.m. Fifteen minutes were allowed for this train to set down and pick up wagons, after which it returned to Eastbourne. The daily through goods to Tunbridge Wells, at this period, left Eastbourne at 10.18 a.m. and, after spending just over an hour at Polegate, conveyed wagons for all stations to Tunbridge Wells except Hellingly. Its arrival at Heathfield, where the engine of the Rotherfield goods was still working, was at 12.45 p.m. and for twenty minutes there were two goods trains at the station. The through goods continued on its way at 1.05 p.m. and at 1.25 p.m. the Rotherfield goods departed for Eastbourne with ten minutes allowed at Waldron and half an hour at Hellingly for shunting.

After an hour and twenty minutes at Polegate, its arrival at Eastbourne was at 4.15 p.m. Meanwhile the through goods arrival at Tunbridge Wells was at 3.47 p.m., after time allowed at all stations. The return working began at 4.25 p.m. and, with time allowed at all stations except Groombridge and Hellingly, its arrival at Polegate was at 7.55 p.m. The engine then ran light to Eastbourne. An important part of the goods traffic at this period was the carriage of livestock and there were special arrangements on the Hailsham cattle market days for horse-boxes and cattle vans. Provided they were vacuum brake fitted they could be attached to the 12.40 p.m. passenger train from Eastbourne to Tunbridge Wells, the engine of the 12.30 p.m. train from Polegate to Hailsham doing the necessary shunting.

Apart from the changes of 1914 which have already been referred to, the timetables continued to be much the same until the last two years of the separate existence of the LBSCR. Then, for the first time since the full opening of the line, the daily through goods was not included in the timetable of 1921. This was probably due

to engineering work taking place in Oxted tunnel which was open for single line working at certain times of the day only. This caused widespread alterations to the time-tables and normal services were not resumed until October 1922. During this period most trains which would have used the Oxted route, including those from Brighton and Eastbourne, were diverted through East Grinstead and Three Bridges. Other passenger services from Eastbourne to Tunbridge Wells were not affected but what would have been the through goods worked only as far as Rother-field where it met the Tunbridge Wells to Lewes goods train which had been diverted from Eridge. Loaded wagons for Tunbridge Wells were conveyed by this train, back to

LONDON TO EASTBOURNE & TUNBRIDGE WELLS TO EASTBOURNE — 1921 DOWN

[Detailed railway timetable — columns for multiple PASS and GOODS services with arr/dep times for stations: Tunbridge Wells, High Rocks Halt, Groombridge, Birchden Junct, Eridge, Redgate Mill Jn, Rotherfield, Mayfield, Heathfield, Waldron, Hellingly, Hailsham, Polegate, Hampden Park, Eastbourne. Includes notes H, V and Sundays and Good Friday — 1921 section.]

EASTBOURNE TO TUNBRIDGE WELLS & EASTBOURNE TO LONDON — 1921 UP

[Detailed railway timetable — columns for GOODS and multiple PASS services with arr/dep times for stations: Eastbourne, Hampden Park, Polegate, Hailsham, Hellingly, Waldron, Heathfield, Mayfield, Rotherfield, Redgate Mill Jn, Eridge, Birchden Junct, Groombridge, High Rocks Halt, Tunbridge Wells. Includes notes H, V, A and Sundays and Good Friday — 1921 section.]

Eridge where they were attached to an up goods train from the Uckfield line. When normal workings were resumed in 1922, however, the down through goods became a Tunbridge Wells working and departed from Tunbridge Wells before the up goods had arrived. The first Southern Railway Goods Timetable of October 1923 was very similar to the LBSCR one of 1922 and was as follows:

Working No. 177	Polegate	Depart	8.35 a.m.
	Tunbridge Wells	Arrive	1.12 p.m.
Working No. 179	Polegate	Depart	1.22 p.m.
	Heathfield	Arrive	3.17 p.m.
	Heathfield	Depart	5.00 p.m.
	Polegate	Arrive	6.40 p.m.
Working No. 93a	Tunbridge Wells	Depart	12.30 p.m.
	Polegate	Arrive	4.40 p.m.

There was no Hellingly goods at this time but it had been restored to the timetable by 1927, which was as follows:

Working No. 177	Polegate	Depart	7.10 a.m.
	Tunbridge Wells	Arrive	12.02 p.m.
Working No. 178	Polegate	Depart	8.55 a.m.
	Hellingly	Arrive	9.35 a.m.
	Hellingly	Depart	9.51 a.m.
	Polegate	Arrive	10.50 a.m.
Working No. 179	Polegate	Depart	11.30 a.m.
	Heathfield	Arrive	1.22 p.m.
	Heathfield	Depart	3.05 p.m.
	Polegate	Arrive	4.06 p.m.
Working No. 105	Tunbridge Wells	Depart	2.50 p.m.
	Polegate	Arrive	7.35 p.m.

By 1929 the down goods from Tunbridge Wells had become part of working number 177 and once again an Eastbourne responsibility.

Reference has already been made to the special arrangements for milk traffic from Mayfield on Sundays and by the late 1920s milk traffic had become an increasingly important source of revenue until it was eventually lost to road transport. From 1929 milk vans from Waldron were attached to the 8.20 p.m. passenger train from Heathfield to Eastbourne, except during 1934 when a special milk train left Waldron at 8.20 p.m.; the Heathfield to Eastbourne train being re-timed to leave at 8.27 p.m. Curiously the working timetable gave no indication of a balancing working for the milk train. There were instructions in the 1931 edition of the timetable for the through goods, departing from Polegate at 7.10 a.m. to convey empty milk vans off the 2.00 a.m. milk train from New Cross which arrived at Polegate at 6.25 a.m. Further references to the milk traffic at Waldron and Mayfield are made in the chapters dealing with those stations.

The year 1938 saw the introduction of an early morning passenger and van train leaving Eastbourne at 5.43 a.m. and stopping at all stations to Waldron, by now renamed Horam, where it arrived at 6.25 a.m. At 6.40 a.m. it returned, as a van train, to Hailsham where it arrived at 6.52 a.m. This arrangement continued into 1939 and the same timings still applied in 1947 although the descriptions had been reversed with the down train becoming the passenger and van train and stopping at

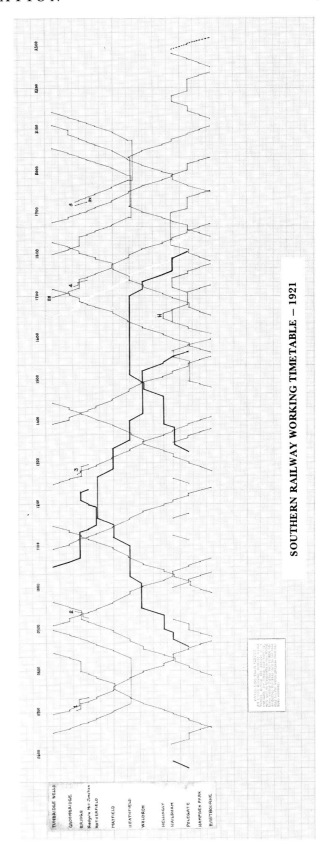

SOUTHERN RAILWAY WORKING TIMETABLE – 1921

TUNBRIDGE WELLS TO EASTBOURNE – 1934 DOWN

	PASS		MOTOR TRAIN (NS)		PASS		PASS		PASS	
	arr a.m.	dep	arr a.m.	dep	arr a.m.	dep	arr a.m.	dep	arr a.m.	dep
TUNBRIDGE WELLS				6.30						
High Rocks Halt										
Groombridge			6.36	6.37				7.05		
Birchden Junct			6.39				7.07			
Eridge			6.41				7.09	7.10		
Redgate Mill Jn			6.43	6.43½			7.12	7.13		
Rotherfield			6.47½	6.48			7.17	7.19		
Mayfield			6.56	7.02			7.27	7.35		
Heathfield			7.13				7.46	7.48		
Waldron							7.55	7.57		
Hellingly							8.05	8.07		
Hailsham		7.00				7.35	8.11	8.14		8.40
Polegate	7.07	7.12			7.42	7.43	8.21	8.26	8.47	8.53
Hampden Park	7.16	7.17			7.47	7.48	8.30	8.31	8.57	8.58
EASTBOURNE	7.21				7.52		8.35		9.02	

	MOTOR TRAIN		GOODS No. 210		PASS 7.50 a.m. Redhill		LIGHT ENGINE off No. 210		PASS	
	arr a.m.	dep	arr a.m.	dep	arr a.m.	dep	arr a.m.	dep	arr a.m.	dep
TUNBRIDGE WELLS					8.49	9.06				
High Rocks Halt										
Groombridge					9.12	9.13				
Birchden Junct					9.15					
Eridge					9.17	9.18				
Redgate Mill Jn					9.20	9.21				
Rotherfield					9.25	9.26		10.35		
Mayfield					9.34	9.35	10.43	10.58		
Heathfield					9.46	9.47	11.10			
Waldron					9.55	10.03				
Hellingly				9.51	10.10	10.11				
Hailsham		9.37	9.56	10.40	10.15	10.16				11.26
Polegate	9.44	9.51	10.50		10.23	10.17			11.33	11.36
Hampden Park	9.55	9.56			10.31	10.32			11.40	11.41
EASTBOURNE	10.00				10.36				11.45	

	PASS		PASS 11.15 a.m. Victoria		PASS		PASS (NS)		PASS	
	arr a.m.	dep	arr p.m.	dep	arr p.m.	dep	arr p.m.	dep	arr p.m.	dep
TUNBRIDGE WELLS		10.42								
High Rocks Halt										
Groombridge	10.48	10.49								
Birchden Junct	10.51		12.19							
Eridge	10.53	10.54	12.21	12.24						
Redgate Mill Jn	10.56	10.57	12.26	12.27						
Rotherfield	11.01	11.08	12.31	12.32						
Mayfield	11.16	11.18	12.40	12.41						
Heathfield	11.29	11.32	12.52	12.53						
Waldron	11.40	11.41	1.01	1.02						
Hellingly	11.48	11.49	1.09	1.10						
Hailsham	11.53	11.54	1.14	1.16		1.45		2.02		2.25
Polegate	12.01	12.03	1.23	1.32	1.52	1.53	2.09	2.10	2.32	
Hampden Park	12.07	12.08	1.36	1.37	1.57	1.58	2.14	2.15		
EASTBOURNE	12.12		1.41		2.02		2.19			

	PASS		GOODS No. 211		GOODS (SO) No. 209		GOODS (NS) No. 209		PASS	
	arr p.m.	dep	arr p.m.	dep	arr p.m.	dep	arr p.m.	dep	arr p.m.	dep
TUNBRIDGE WELLS		1.57				2.45		2.45		
High Rocks Halt										
Groombridge	2.03	2.04			2.54		2.54			
Birchden Junct	2.06									
Eridge	2.08	2.10			2.59		3.00			
Redgate Mill Jn	2.12	2.13			3.02	3.03	3.04	3.05		
Rotherfield	2.17	2.18			3.10	3.20	3.15	3.28		
Mayfield	2.26	2.27			3.30	3.50	3.38	3.55		
Heathfield	2.38	2.39		2.50	4.05	4.20	4.10	4.45		
Waldron	2.47	2.48	2.59	3.10	4.30	5.18	5.00	5.50		
Hellingly	2.55	2.56	3.20	3.25						
Hailsham	3.00	3.02	3.30	3.55	5.32	6.14	6.05	7.20		3.26
Polegate	3.09	3.10	4.05		6.24		7.30		3.33	3.40
Hampden Park	3.14	3.15							3.44	3.45
EASTBOURNE	3.19								3.45	

	PASS		PASS		PASS 3.06 p.m. Redhill		PASS		PASS	
	arr p.m.	dep	arr p.m.	dep	arr p.m.	dep	arr p.m.	dep	arr p.m.	dep
TUNBRIDGE WELLS					4.10	4.25				5.55
High Rocks Halt										
Groombridge					4.31	4.33			6.01	6.02
Birchden Junct					4.36				6.04	
Eridge					4.36 v	4.50			6.06	6.11
Redgate Mill Jn					4.52	4.53			6.13	6.14
Rotherfield					4.57	4.58			6.19	6.20
Mayfield					5.06	5.08			6.27	6.28
Heathfield					5.19	5.26			6.39	6.40
Waldron	H				5.33	5.34			6.47	6.48
Hellingly					5.41	5.42			6.56	6.57
Hailsham		4.33		5.22	5.46	5.47		6.41	7.01	7.02
Polegate	4.40	4.50	5.29	5.32	5.54	5.55	6.48	6.50	7.09	7.11
Hampden Park	4.54	4.55	5.36	5.37	5.59	6.00	6.54	6.55	7.15	7.16
EASTBOURNE	4.59		5.41		6.04		6.59		7.20	

H: On Tuesdays and Saturdays, also on alternate Wednesdays (Asylum Visiting Days only) starts from Hellingly at 4.28 p.m. and calls at Hailsham 4.32 – 4.33 p.m.

V: Through carriages off 3.45 p.m. Victoria attached at Eridge

	PASS		MILK		PASS (NS)		PASS		MOTOR TRAIN (NWS)	
	arr p.m.	dep	arr p.m.	dep	arr p.m.	dep	arr p.m.	dep	arr p.m.	dep
TUNBRIDGE WELLS		6.58								
High Rocks Halt										
Groombridge	7.04	7.05								
Birchden Junct	7.07									
Eridge	7.09 v	7.21								
Redgate Mill Jn	7.23	7.24								
Rotherfield	7.28	7.29								
Mayfield	7.37	7.38								
Heathfield	7.49	7.52				8.27				
Waldron	8.00	8.05		8.20	8.35	8.36				
Hellingly	8.13	8.14	8.28		8.44	8.45				
Hailsham	8.18	8.21	8.32	8.33	8.49	8.51		9.05		9.50
Polegate	8.28	8.32	8.41	8.46	8.58	9.03	9.12	9.13	9.57	10.04
Hampden Park	8.36	8.37			9.07	9.08	9.17	9.18	10.08	10.09
EASTBOURNE	8.41		8.54		9.12		9.22		10.13	

V: Through carriages off 6.10 p.m. Victoria attached at Eridge

	PASS (NS)		PASS (SO)		MOTOR TRAIN (WSO)		ENGINE		ENGINE	
	arr p.m.	dep	arr p.m.	dep	arr p.m.	dep	arr p.m.	dep	arr p.m.	dep
TUNBRIDGE WELLS		8.48		9.30						
High Rocks Halt										
Groombridge	8.54	8.55	9.36	9.39						
Birchden Junct	8.57		9.41							
Eridge	8.59	9.09	9.43	9.44						
Redgate Mill Jn	9.11	9.12	9.46	9.47						
Rotherfield	9.16	9.17	9.51	9.51½						
Mayfield	9.25	9.26	9.59	10.00						
Heathfield	9.37	9.43	10.11	10.12		10.42				
Waldron	9.51	9.52	10.20	10.20½	10.50	10.51				
Hellingly	10.00	10.01	10.27½	10.28	10.59	11.00				
Hailsham	10.05	10.06	10.32	10.34	11.04	11.05		11.15		12.00
Polegate	10.13	10.20	10.41	10.43	11.12	11.14	11.22		12.07	
Hampden Park	10.24	10.25	10.47	10.48	11.18	11.19				
EASTBOURNE	10.29		10.52		11.23					

SUNDAYS

	PASS		PASS		PASS 8.49 a.m. Tonbridge		PASS		PASS	
	arr a.m.	dep	arr a.m.	dep	arr a.m.	dep	arr a.m.	dep	arr a.m.	dep
TUNBRIDGE WELLS					9.04	9.05				10.20
High Rocks Halt										
Groombridge					9.11	9.12			10.26	10.29
Birchden Junct					9.14				10.31	
Eridge					9.16	9.17			10.33	10.34½
Redgate Mill Jn					9.19	9.20			10.36½	10.37
Rotherfield					9.24	9.25			10.41½	10.42
Mayfield					9.33	9.34			10.50	10.51
Heathfield					9.45	9.46			11.02	11.06
Waldron					9.54	9.55			11.14	11.15
Hellingly					10.03	10.04			11.23	11.24
Hailsham		7.09		10.06	10.09	10.10		10.49	11.28	11.31
Polegate	7.16	7.28	10.13	10.15	10.16	10.17	10.56	10.58	11.38	11.40
Hampden Park	7.32	7.33	10.19	10.20	10.21	10.26	11.02	11.03	11.44	11.45
EASTBOURNE	7.37		10.24		10.30		11.07		11.49	

	PASS		PASS		PASS		PASS		PASS	
	arr p.m.	dep	arr p.m.	dep	arr p.m.	dep	arr p.m.	dep	arr p.m.	dep
TUNBRIDGE WELLS						4.12				
High Rocks Halt										
Groombridge					4.18	4.20				
Birchden Junct					4.22					
Eridge					4.24	4.25				
Redgate Mill Jn					4.27	4.28				
Rotherfield					4.32	4.33				
Mayfield					4.41	4.43				7.17
Heathfield		1.39			4.54	4.55			7.28	7.29
Waldron	1.47	1.48			5.03	5.04			7.37	7.41
Hellingly	1.56	1.57			5.12	5.14			7.50	7.51
Hailsham	2.01	2.02		2.27	5.18	5.19		5.54	7.55	7.56
Polegate	2.09	2.10	2.34	2.35	5.26	5.28	6.01	6.02	8.03	8.07
Hampden Park	2.14	2.15	2.39	2.40	5.32	5.33	6.06	6.07	8.11	8.12
EASTBOURNE	2.19		2.44		5.37		6.11		8.16	

	PASS		PASS		PASS		ENGINE		EMPTY	
	arr p.m.	dep	arr p.m.	dep	arr p.m.	dep	arr p.m.	dep	arr p.m.	dep
TUNBRIDGE WELLS				8.27						
High Rocks Halt										
Groombridge			8.33	8.35						
Birchden Junct			8.37							
Eridge			8.39	8.40						
Redgate Mill Jn			8.42	8.43						
Rotherfield			8.47	8.48						
Mayfield			8.58	9.00						
Heathfield			9.11	9.14		10.13				
Waldron			9.22	9.25	10.21	10.22				
Hellingly			9.33	9.34	10.30	10.31				
Hailsham		8.50	9.39	9.42	10.36	10.42		10.55		11.27
Polegate	8.57	9.04	9.49	9.50	10.49	10.50	11.02		11.34	
Hampden Park	9.08	9.09	9.54	9.55	10.54	10.55				
EASTBOURNE	9.13		9.59		10.59					

EASTBOURNE TO TUNBRIDGE WELLS – 1934 UP

	ENGINE		PASS		GOODS No. 209		MOTOR TRAIN (NS)		PASS		PASS	
	arr a.m.	dep	arr a.m.	dep	arr a.m.	dep	arr a.m.	dep	arr a.m.	dep	arr a.m.	dep
EASTBOURNE		6.20		6.37						7.51		8.15
Hampden Park			6.41	6.42					7.55	7.56	8.19	8.20
Polegate	6.28	6.30	6.46	6.48		7.10			8.00	8.03	8.24	8.25
Hailsham	6.37		6.55	6.56	7.19	7.27			8.10	8.16	8.32	
Hellingly			7.00	7.01	7.32				8.20	8.22		
Waldron			7.09	7.10	7.42	8.12			8.30	8.33		
Heathfield			7.18	7.19	8.24	9.12		8.10	8.41	8.44		
Mayfield			7.30	7.41	9.24	10.05	8.21	8.22	8.55	8.57		
Rotherfield			7.49	7.52	10.15	12.00	8.29	8.30	9.04	9.05		
Redgate Mill Jn			7.56	7.57	12.04	12.06	8.33	8.34	9.08	9.09		
Eridge			7.59	8.11	12.10	12.16	8.36	8.47	9.11 v	9.25		
Birchden Junct			8.13		12.18		8.49		9.27			
Groombridge			8.15	8.17	12.22	12.41	8.51	8.52	9.29	9.30		
High Rocks Halt												
TUNBRIDGE WELLS			8.23	8.27	12.54		8.58		9.36			
			↓ to Guildford via Tonbridge						V: Through carriages to Victoria detached at Eridge			

	MOTOR TRAIN		GOODS No. 210		PASS		MOTOR TRAIN		ENGINE off No. 209		GOODS No. 211	
	arr a.m.	dep	arr a.m.	dep	arr a.m.	dep	arr a.m.	dep	arr a.m.	dep	arr a.m.	dep
EASTBOURNE		8.50				9.50		10.59				
Hampden Park	8.54	8.55			9.54	9.55	11.03	11.04				
Polegate	8.59	9.07		9.55	9.59	10.03	11.08	11.13				11.35
Hailsham	9.14		9.04	9.30	10.10	10.19	11.20				11.44	12.00
Hellingly			9.35		10.23	10.24					12.04	12.42
Waldron					10.32	10.35					12.52	1.10
Heathfield					10.42	10.45				11.32	1.22	
Mayfield					10.56	10.58						
Rotherfield					11.05	11.06			11.47			
Redgate Mill Jn					11.09	11.10						
Eridge					11.12v	11.15						
Birchden Junct					11.17							
Groombridge					11.19	11.20						
High Rocks Halt												
TUNBRIDGE WELLS					11.26	11.28						
					↓ to Tonbridge							

	PASS		PASS		PASS (NS)		PASS		PASS		PASS	
	arr p.m.	dep	arr p.m.	dep	arr p.m.	dep	arr p.m.	dep	arr p.m.	dep	arr p.m.	dep
EASTBOURNE		12.14		12.55		1.18		2.00				3.34
Hampden Park	12.18	12.19	12.59	1.00	1.22	1.23	2.04	2.05			3.38	3.39
Polegate	12.23	12.24	1.04	1.05	1.27	1.32	2.09	2.11		3.13	3.43	3.44
Hailsham	12.31		1.12	1.19	1.39		2.18		3.20		3.51	3.52
Hellingly			1.23	1.24							3.56	3.57
Waldron			1.32	1.36							4.05	4.06
Heathfield			1.43	1.45							4.13	4.16
Mayfield			1.56	1.57							4.20	4.27
Rotherfield			2.04	2.05							4.33	4.33H
Redgate Mill Jn			2.08	2.09							4.36H	4.37
Eridge			2.11	2.12							4.40	4.47
Birchden Junct			2.14								4.50	
Groombridge											4.52	4.54
High Rocks Halt												
TUNBRIDGE WELLS											5.00	5.04
			↓ to Victoria								↓ to Tonbridge	

H: On Tuesdays & Saturdays also on alternate Wednesdays (Asylum visiting days) runs on to Hellingly Dep Hailsham 4.15 p.m. arr Hellingly 4.19 p.m.

	PASS		PASS		PASS		PASS		PASS		PASS		MOTOR TRAIN	
	arr p.m.	dep	arr p.m.	dep	arr p.m.	dep	arr p.m.	dep	arr p.m.	dep	arr p.m.	dep	arr p.m.	dep
EASTBOURNE		3.55		4.40		4.50		5.50		6.17		6.40		7.30
Hampden Park	3.59	4.00	4.44	4.45	4.54	4.55	5.54	5.55	6.21	6.22	6.44	6.45	7.34	7.35
Polegate	4.04	4.06	4.49	4.51	4.59	5.05	5.59	6.02	6.26	6.27	6.49	6.50	7.39	7.41
Hailsham	4.13		4.58	5.00	5.12		6.09	6.10	6.34		6.57	7.04	7.48	7.49
Hellingly			5.04	5.05			6.14	6.15			7.08	7.09	7.53	7.54
Waldron	H		5.14	5.16			6.23	6.30			7.17	7.18	8.02	8.10
Heathfield			5.23	5.30			6.38	6.43			7.26		8.17	8.18
Mayfield			5.41	5.45			6.54	6.55					8.29	8.30
Rotherfield			5 52	5.55½			7.03	7.05					8.37	8.38
Redgate Mill Jn			5.58½	5.59			7.08	7.09					8.42	8.43
Eridge			6.01	6.02			7.11	7.17					8.45	8.46
Birchden Junct			6.04				7.20						8.48	
Groombridge			6.06	6.07			7.22	7.23					8.50	8.54
High Rocks Halt														
TUNBRIDGE WELLS			6.13				7.29						9.00	9.02
													↓ to Tonbridge	

	PASS		MOTOR TRAIN (NWS)		MOTOR TRAIN (WSO)		PASS		PASS	
	arr p.m.	dep	arr p.m.	dep	arr p.m.	dep	arr p.m.	dep	arr p.m.	dep
EASTBOURNE		8.00		9.15		9.15		10.40		11.30
Hampden Park	8.04	8.05	9.19	9.20	9.19	9.20	10.44	10.45	11.34	11.35
Polegate	8.09	8.10	9.24	9.26	9.24	9.26	10.49	10.50	11.39	11.40
Hailsham	8.17		9.33		9.33	9.34	10.57		11.47	
Hellingly					9.38	9.39				
Waldron					9.47	9.54				
Heathfield					10.01					
Mayfield										
Rotherfield										
Redgate Mill Jn										
Eridge										
Birchden Junct										
Groombridge										
High Rocks Halt										
TUNBRIDGE WELLS										

SUNDAYS

	ENGINE		PASS		PASS		PASS		PASS		PASS		PASS	
	arr a.m.	dep	arr a.m.	dep	arr a.m.	dep	arr a.m.	dep	arr a.m.	dep	arr p.m.	dep	arr p.m.	dep
EASTBOURNE		6.45		7.08		9.42		10.16		12.45		2.00		5.00
Hampden Park			7.12	7.13	9.46	9.47	10.20	10.25	12.49	12.50	2.04	2.05	5.04	5.05
Polegate	6.53	6.54	7.17	7.22	9.51	9.52	10.29	10.31	12.54	12.55	2.09	2.12	5.09	5.10
Hailsham	7.01		7.29	7.30	9.59		10.38	10.39	1.02	1.03	2.19		5.17	
Hellingly			7.34	7.36			10.43	10.44	1.07	1.08				
Waldron			7.44	7.50			10.52	10.55	1.16	1.17				
Heathfield			7.57	8.00			11.03	11.09	1.24					
Mayfield			8.11	8.14			11.20	11.21						
Rotherfield			8.22	8.23			11.29	11.30						
Redgate Mill Jn			8.27	8.28			11.34	11.35						
Eridge			8.30	8.31			11.38	11.39						
Birchden Junct			8.33				11.41							
Groombridge			8.35	8.37			11.43	11.44						
High Rocks Halt														
TUNBRIDGE WELLS			8.43				11.50							

	PASS		PASS		PASS		PASS		PASS		PASS		MOTOR TRAIN			
	arr p.m.	dep	arr p.m.	dep	arr p.m.	dep	arr p.m.	dep	arr p.m.	dep	arr p.m.	dep	arr p.m.	dep	arr p.m.	dep
EASTBOURNE		5.29		6.13		7.05		8.18		9.21		10.18		11.00		
Hampden Park	5.33	5.34	6.17	7.18	7.09	7.10	8.22	8.23	9.25	9.26	10.22	10.23	11.04	11.05		
Polegate	5.38	5.39	6.22	6.24	7.14	7.16	8.27	8.28	9.30	9.31	10.27	10.31	11.09	11.10		
Hailsham	5.46	5.47	6.31	6.32	7.23	7.24	8.35		9.38	9.43	10.38		11.17			
Hellingly	5.51	5.52	6.36	6.37	7.28	7.29			9.47	9.48						
Waldron	6.00	6.14	6.45	6.46	7.37	7.41			9.56	9.58						
Heathfield	6.22	6.26	6.54	6.56	7.49	7.50			10.05							
Mayfield	6.37		7 07	7.12	8.01	8.02										
Rotherfield			7.20	7.21	8.10	8.11										
Redgate Mill Jn			7.25	7.26	8.15	8.16										
Eridge			7.39	7.30	8.18	8.19										
Birchden Junct			7.32		8.21											
Groombridge			7.35	7.37	8.24	8.25										
High Rocks Halt																
TUNBRIDGE WELLS			7.43	7.56	8.31	8.35										
			↓ to Redhill via Tonbridge		↓ to Tonbridge											

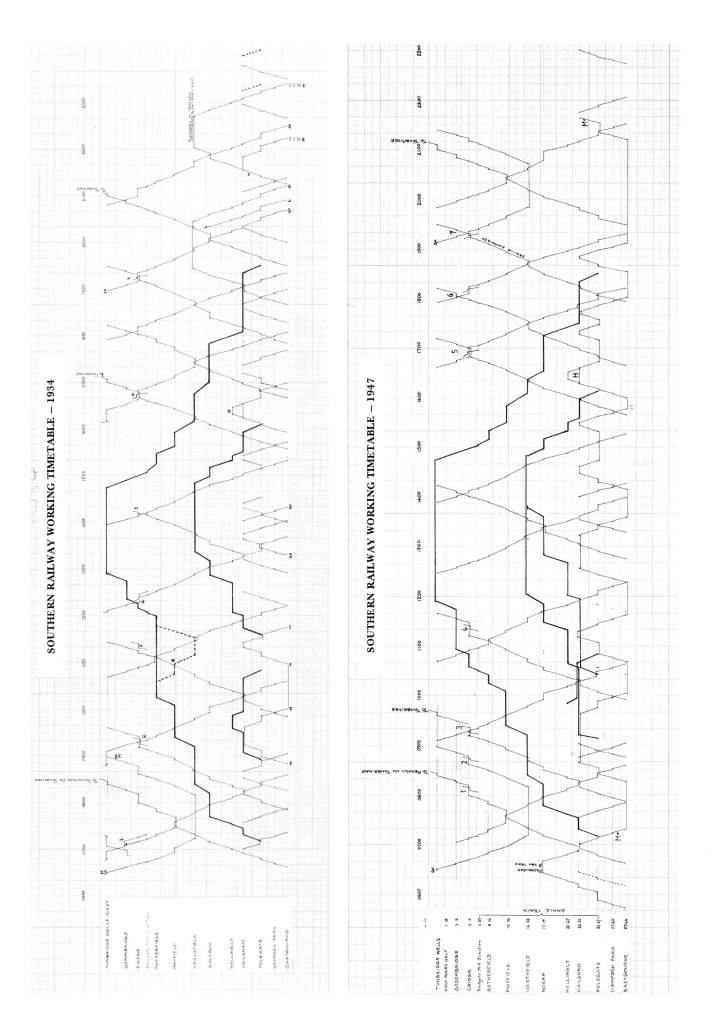

SOUTHERN RAILWAY WORKING TIMETABLE – 1934

SOUTHERN RAILWAY WORKING TIMETABLE – 1947

TUNBRIDGE WELLS TO EASTBOURNE – 1947 DOWN

	PASS		PASS & VANS		MOTOR TRAIN		PASS		PASS		PASS		MOTOR TRAIN		GOODS (SX)		PASS	
	arr a.m.	dep	arr a.m.	dep	arr a.m.	dep	arr a.m.	dep	arr a.m.	dep	arr a.m.	dep	arr a.m.	dep	arr a.m.	dep	arr a.m.	dep
TUNBRIDGE WELLS		6.30																9.06
High Rocks Halt																		
Groombridge	6.36	6.37								7.02							9.12	9.13
Birchden Junct	6.39								7.04								9.15	
Eridge	6.41	6.42							7.06	7.08							9.17	9.18
Redgate Mill Jn	6.44	6.45							7.10	7.11							9.20	9.21
Rotherfield	6.49	6.50							7.15	7.17							9.25	9.26
Mayfield	7.10								7.25	7.35							9.34	9.35
Heathfield									7.46	7.48							9.46	9.47
Waldron				6.40					7.55	7.57							9.55	10.03
Hellingly			6.47	6.48					8.05	8.07						9.51	10.10	10.10½
Hailsham			6.52			7.00		7.33	8.11	8.14		8.45		9.38	9.56	10.40	10.14½	10.16
Polegate					7.07	7.09	7.40	7.41	8.21	8.26	8.52	8.52½	9.45	9.53	10.50		10.23	10.29
Hampden Park					7.13	7.14	7.45	7.46	8.30	8.31	8.56½	8.57	9.57	9.58			10.33	10.34
EASTBOURNE					7.19		7.50		8.35		9.01		10.02				10.38	

	PASS		MOTOR TRAIN		MOTOR TRAIN		PASS		PASS		GOODS (SO)		MOTOR TRAIN		PASS		GOODS (SX)	
	arr a.m.	dep	arr a.m.	dep	arr a.m.	dep	arr p.m.	dep	arr p.m.	dep	arr p.m.	dep	arr p.m.	dep	arr p.m.	dep	arr p.m.	dep
TUNBRIDGE WELLS		10.42						12.28								1.54		
High Rocks Halt																		
Groombridge	10.48	10.50					12.34	12.36							2.00	2.01		
Birchden Junct	10.52						12.38								2.03			
Eridge	10.54	10.55					12.40	12.41							2.05	2.08		
Redgate Mill Jn	10.57	10.58					12.43	12.44							2.10	2.11		
Rotherfield	11.02	11.08					12.48	12.49							2.15	2.16		
Mayfield	11.16	11.18					12.57	12.59							2.24	2.25		
Heathfield	11.29	11.34					1.10	1.12				1.35			2.36	2.37		2.50
Waldron	11.41	11.42					1.20	1.23			1.44	1.50			2.45	2.46	2.59	3.10
Hellingly	11.49	11.50					1.30	1.31			2.00	2.10			2.53	2.54	3.20	3.30
Hailsham	11.54	11.55		11.19		1.14	1.35	1.37		2.00	2.15	2.45		3.37	2.58	2.59	3.35	3.59
Polegate	12.02	12.07	11.26	11.28	1.21	1.26	1.44	1.50	2.07	2L07½	2.55		2.44		3.06	3L07	4.08	
Hampden Park	12.11	12.12	11.32	11.33	1.30½	1.31	1.54	1.55	2L11½	2L12					3L11	3L12		
EASTBOURNE	12.16		11.37		1.35		1.59		2L16						3L16			
	Suspended								L: 6 mins later on Saturdays						L: 7 mins later on Saturdays			

	GOODS		MOTOR TRAIN		MOTOR TRAIN		MOTOR TRAIN		MOTOR TRAIN		PASS		MOTOR TRAIN		PASS		PASS (SX)		PASS		MOTOR TRAIN (SX)	
	arr p.m.	dep	arr p.m.	dep	arr p.m.	dep	arr p.m.	dep	arr p.m.	dep	arr p.m.	dep	arr p.m.	dep	arr p.m.	dep	arr p.m.	dep	arr p.m.	dep	arr p.m.	dep
TUNBRIDGE WELLS		2.45										4.37				5.55		7.08		7.50		
High Rocks Halt																						
Groombridge	2.53										4.43	4.45			6.01	6.02	7.14	7.15	7.56	7.58		
Birchden Junct	2.56										4.47				6.04		7.17		8.00			
Eridge	2.58										4.49 V	5.00½			6.06	6.14	7.19	7.21	8.02	8.03		
Redgate Mill Jn	3.02	3.03									5.02½	5.03			6.16	6.16½	7.23	7.24	8.05	8.06		
Rotherfield	3.10	3.20									5.07½	5.08½			6.20½	6.21	7.28	7.29	8.10	8.11		
Mayfield	3.30	3.50									5.16	5.17			6.29	6.30	7.37	7.39	8.19	8.26		
Heathfield	4.05	4.22									5.28	5.29½			6.41	6.43	7.50		8.37	8.39		
Waldron	4.32	5.15			H						5.36½	5.37½			6.49½	6.50½			8.47	8.56		
Hellingly								5.21		5.44	5.44½	5.45½			6.57	6.57½			9.04	9.05		
Hailsham	5.30	6†20		3.30		4.36	5.28		5.51	5.52	5.49½	5.52		6†51	7.01½	7.02½			9.09	9.11	9.45	
Polegate	6†30		3.37	3.37½	4.43				5.56	5.57	5.59	6.05	6†58	6†58½	7.09½	7.11			9.17	9.22	9.52	9.54
Hampden Park			3.41½	3.42					6.01				7.02½	7.03					9.26	9.27	9.58	9.59
EASTBOURNE			3.46								6.12		7.13		7.18				9.31		10.03	

† 1 hr 5 mins later if required (Goods)

H: On Tuesdays and Saturdays, also on alternate Wednesdays (Asylum Visiting Days only) starts from Hellingly at 4.31 p.m. calls at Hailsham 4.35 – 4.36 p.m.

V: Through carriages off 3.55 Victoria attached at Eridge. Saturday times vary slightly

† 1 minute earlier on Saturdays (Motor Train)

SUNDAYS

	PASS		PASS		PASS		PASS		PASS		PASS	
	arr a.m.	dep	arr a.m.	dep	arr a.m.	dep	arr p.m.	dep	arr p.m.	dep	arr p.m.	dep
TUNBRIDGE WELLS						10.20						8.27
High Rocks Halt					10.23	10.24					8.30	8.31
Groombridge					10.28	10.29					8.34	8.36
Birchden Junct					10.31						8.38	
Eridge					10.33	10.36					8.40	8.41
Redgate Mill Jn					10.38	10.38½					8.43	8.44
Rotherfield					10.42½	10.43					8.48	8.49
Mayfield					10.51	10.52					8.57	8.58
Heathfield		8.45			11.03	11.05		1.35			9.09	9.10
Waldron	8.53	8.54			11.13	11.18	1.43	1.44			9.18	9.26
Hellingly	9.01	9.01½			11.25	11.26	1.52	1.53			9.34	9.35
Hailsham	9.05½	9.06½		10.12	11.30	11.31	1.57	1.58		8.45	9.40	9.41
Polegate	9.13½	9.14½	10.19	10.22	11.38	11.39	2.05	2.06	8.52	8.54	9.48	9.58
Hampden Park	9.18½	9.19	10.26	10.27			2.10	2.11	8.58	8.59	10.02	10.03
EASTBOURNE	9.23		10.31		11.46		2.15		9.03		10.07	

EASTBOURNE TO TUNBRIDGE WELLS – 1947 UP

	VANS		ENGINE		PASS		PASS (SX)		GOODS		PASS		PASS		MOTOR TRAIN	
	arr a.m.	dep	arr a.m.	dep	arr a.m.	dep	arr a.m.	dep	arr a.m.	dep	arr a.m.	dep	arr a.m.	dep	arr a.m.	dep
EASTBOURNE		5.43		6.10		6.37						7.52		8.16		8.45
Hampden Park	5.47	5.48			6.41	6.42					7.56	7.57	8.20	8.21	8.49	8.50
Polegate	5.52	6.02	6.18	6.20	6.46	6.48				7.10	8.01	8.02	8.25	8.32	8.54	8.55
Hailsham	6.09	6.12½	6.27		6.55	6.57			7.19	7.32	8.09	8.16	8.39		9.02	
Hellingly	6.16½	6.17			7.01	7.02			7.37		8.20	8.22				
Waldron	6.25				7.10	7.12			7.47	8.12	8.30	8.33				
Heathfield					7.20	7.21		8.10	8.24	9.12	8.41	8.44				
Mayfield					7.32	7.41	8.21	8.21½	9.24	10.05	8.55	8.57				
Rotherfield					7.49	7.52	8.29	8.29½	10.15	10.25	9.04	9.05				
Redgate Mill Jn					7.56	7.57	8.33	8.33½	10.30	10.31	9.08	9.09				
Eridge					7.59	8.11	8.36	8.37	10.35	10.50	9.11 V					
Birchden Junct					8.13		8.39		10.52							
Groombridge					8.15	8.17	8.51	8.52	10.56	11.44						
High Rocks Halt																
TUNBRIDGE WELLS					8.23	8.26	8.58		11.54							
					to Redhill via Tonbridge						V: Attached to 8 a.m. Brighton to Victoria				Calls at No. 73 Gates (between Polegate & Hailsham) to put down cans of water	

	GOODS		PASS		GOODS (SX) If required		MOTOR TRAIN		GOODS (SX) If required		MOTOR TRAIN		PASS		PASS		MOTOR TRAIN		MOTOR TRAIN	
	arr a.m.	dep	arr a.m.	dep	arr a.m.	dep	arr a.m.	dep	arr a.m.	dep	arr p.m.	dep	arr p.m.	dep	arr p.m.	dep	arr p.m.	dep	arr p.m.	dep
EASTBOURNE				9.55				10.41				12.17		12.45		1.17		2.09		
Hampden Park							10.45	10.46			12.21	12.21½	12.49	12.50	1.21	1.21½	2.13	2.13½		
Polegate		9L08	10.04	10.05		10.25	10.50	11.04		11.31	12.25½	12.26	12.54	12.55	1.25½	1.26	2.17½	2.21		3.19
Hailsham	9.12	10.34	10.12	10.18½	10.34	10.36	11.11		11.40	12.00	12.33		1.02	1.04	1.33		2.28		3.26	
Hellingly	10.39	11.19	10.22½	10.23	12.01	12.40			12.04	12.42			1.08	1.09						
Waldron	11.29	11.50	10.31	10.34	12.50	1.35			12.52	1.00			1.17	1.25						
Heathfield	12.02		10.41	10.44	1.47				1.10				1.32	1.34						
Mayfield			10.55	10.57									1.45	1.46						
Rotherfield			11.04	11.06									1.53	1.54						
Redgate Mill Jn			11.09	11.10									1.57	1.58						
Eridge			11.12	11.28									2.00	2.01						
Birchden Junct			11.30										2.03							
Groombridge			11.32	11.33									2.05	2.07						
High Rocks Halt																				
TUNBRIDGE WELLS			11.39										2.13							
	L: 12 mins later between Polegate & Hailsham on Sats																			

	PASS		MOTOR TRAIN		PASS		MOTOR TRAIN		MOTOR TRAIN		PASS		MOTOR TRAIN		PASS		PASS		MOTOR TRAIN (SX)		PASS	
	arr p.m.	dep	arr p.m.	dep	arr p.m.	dep	arr p.m.	dep	arr p.m.	dep	arr p.m.	dep	arr p.m.	dep	arr p.m.	dep	arr p.m.	dep	arr p.m.	dep	arr p.m.	dep
EASTBOURNE		3.39		4.00		4.39						5.56		6.32		7.29				9.12		10.44
Hampden Park	3.43	3.44	4.04	4.05	4.43	4.44													9.16	9.16½	10.48	10.49
Polegate	3.48	3.50	4.09	4.10	4.48	4.51		5.10		5.34	6.03	6.05	6.39	6E41	7.36	7.40			9.20½	9.32	10.53	10.54
Hailsham	3.57	3.58	4.17	4H18	4.58	5.00	5.17		5.41		6.12	6.15	6E48 ↓		7.47	7.49			9.39		11.01	
Hellingly	4.02	4.03	4H22 ↓		5.04	5.05					6.19	6.20			7.53	7.54						
Waldron	4.11	4.12			5.14	5.16					6.28	6.30			8.02	8.04						
Heathfield	4.20	4.22			5.23	5.32					6.38	6.45			8.11	8.13		8.43				
Mayfield	4.33	4.34			5.43	5.43½					6.56	6.57			8.24	8.29	8.54	8.55				
Rotherfield	4.41	4.42			5.51	5.51½					7.05	7.06			8.36	8.38	9.02	9.03				
Redgate Mill Jn	4.45	4.45½			5.54½	5.55					7.10	7.11			8.42	8.43	9.07	9.08				
Eridge	4.48	5.00			5.57½	5.58½					7.13	7.17			8.45	8.46	9.10	9.13				
Birchden Junct	5.02				6.00½						7.20				8.48		9.15					
Groombridge	5.04	5.05			6.02½	6.06					7.22	7.23			8.50	8.54	9.17	9.18				
High Rocks Halt																						
TUNBRIDGE WELLS	5.11				6.12						7.29 ↓ Suspended				9.00	9.05 ↓ to Tonbridge	9.24					

H: Tues & Sats also alternate Wednesdays (Asylum visiting days only)

E: 1 minute earlier on Saturdays

SUNDAYS

	PASS & VANS		PASS		PASS		PASS		PASS		PASS	
	arr a.m.	dep	arr a.m.	dep	arr a.m.	dep	arr p.m.	dep	arr p.m.	dep	arr p.m.	dep
EASTBOURNE				9.46		10.16		12.43		6.16		8.19
Hampden Park			9.50	9.51	10.20	10.21	12.47	12.47½	6.20	6.21	8.23	8.23½
Polegate		7.40	9.55	9.56	10.25	10.31	12.51½	12.55	6.25	6.26	8.27½	8.31
Hailsham	7.47	7.48	10.03		10.38	10.39	1.02	1.03	6.33	6.34	8.37½	
Hellingly	7.52	7.53			10.43	10.44	1.07	1.08	6.38	6.39		
Waldron	8.01				10.52	10.53	1.16	1.17	6.47	6.51		
Heathfield					11.01	11.09	1.24		7.59	7.01		
Mayfield					11.20	11.24			7.11	7.12		
Rotherfield					11.32	11.33			7.20	7.21		
Redgate Mill Jn					11.37	11.38			7.25	7.26		
Eridge					11.41	11.42			7.29	7.30		
Birchden Junct					11.44				7.32			
Groombridge					11.47	11.47½			7.34	7.37		
High Rocks Halt					11.50	11.50½			7.40	7.40½		
TUNBRIDGE WELLS					11.54				7.44	7.50 ↓ to Redhill via Tonbridge		

Hellingly. The 1947 timetable also included an unbalanced goods working from Hellingly at 9.51 a.m., conditional upon requirements, and, in this last year of Southern Railway ownership, the through goods was still leaving Polegate at 7.10 a.m. to arrive at Tunbridge Wells at 11.54 a.m. The return journey began at 2.45 p.m. with arrival at Polegate at 6.30 p.m. There was also a goods working from Polegate to Heathfield and return on Mondays to Fridays with allowance for a second goods to Heathfield if required. Passenger services were much the same as those of forty years earlier and although the Hospital Railway lost its tramcar service in 1931 there was still a passenger train from Eastbourne to Hellingly on hospital visiting days.

1 LBSCR timetables, July/August, 1865.
2   ,,   ,,   July/August, 1885.
3 Half-Yearly Report, LBSCR, January 1894.
4 LBSCR timetables, Summer 1904.
5   ,,   ,,   Summer 1912.
6 White, H. P. Op. Cit. page 95.
7 LBSCR timetables, Summer 1912.
8   ,,   ,,   Summer 1914.
9 The carriages of the train had already worked from London to Redhill.
10 There was a Hastings portion on the early train down and the late train up.
11 Bradley, D. L. Locomotives of the LBSCR, Part 2.

'E4' class 0—6—2 tank No. 2512 approaching Groombridge with a short goods train in March 1948.   *Author's Collection*

This view of the 1897 accident illustrates the sharp curves on the Tunbridge Wells to Eastbourne line.

CHAPTER FOUR

MISHAPS

DURING the eighty-five years of its existence the line had a remarkably good safety record but there was one serious accident and this occurred on 1st September 1897, about two and a half miles north of Heathfield station at a spot known to railwaymen as Tooth's Bank. This was a short level stretch of line at the bottom of gradients rising at one in fifty in each direction, all of which was on a curve of twenty-four chains radius. The accident involved the 8.18 a.m. train from Eastbourne which consisted of six vehicles headed by the D1 class 0—4—2 tank locomotive number 297 *Bonchurch*. In order from the engine, the six vehicles were:

1. Six-wheeled third class coach No. 482   (12 tons 1 cwt)
2. Four-wheeled first and second class composite coach No. 88   (7 tons 16 cwt)
3. Four-wheeled third class brake No. 622   (7 tons 17 cwt)
4. Four-wheeled van No. 217   (7 tons 16 cwt)
5. Six-wheeled first, second and third class composite coach No. 277   (12 tons 5 cwt)
6. Six-wheeled third class brake No. 428   (11 tons 17 cwt)

Three of these coaches were fairly new, No. 482 having been completed in June of the previous year and numbers 277 and 428 being built in June 1894 and December 1895 repectively.

As the train reached the bottom of the dip the engine left the rails and turned over to the right, taking the first carriage with it. The underframe of the second carriage slewed across the top of the embankment while the body slid, on its side, near to the bottom of the slope on the left of the line. The third and fourth carriages went to the bottom of the embankment, more or less on top of each other, and the remaining two carriages also ended up on their sides near the bottom of the slope. The engine stopped in about a hundred yards from the first mark of a wheel being off the track and the permanent way was completely destroyed for a distance of about eighty yards and damaged for a further length of about twenty yards. The driver, James McKinley, was killed almost instantly but the fireman, Lewis Minns, although severely injured, managed to climb out of the cab to find his engine on its side with the wheels still turning slowly. Thirty passengers complained of injury but, as far as was known at the time of the inquiry, few were of a serious nature.

It emerged at the inquiry that the train was running four minutes late and the crew would have been well aware of the importance of making a connection at Groombridge where the last two carriages would be detached to go through to London but the guard, James

'D1' class No. 297 *Bonchurch* lies on one side of the track following the accident on 1st September 1897. The leading coach, which was taken with it, appears to have been removed by the time this photograph was taken.   *John Scrace Collection*

The remainder of the train went over to the other side of the embankment. The underframe of the second coach is clearly visible. 'D3' class No. 381 *Fittleworth* heads the inspection train.   *John Scrace Collection*

Hysom, who was looking out ahead from the left side when his vehicle left the rails, said that he had not noticed anything unusual about the speed of the train. Albert Jay, a line signalman who was on the train and usually travelled the line at least once a day, stated that the road always seemed rough near the point of the accident and particularly when travelling in the northerly direction. It was no more so than usual on this occasion, however, and neither he nor his two fellow travellers who were also railwaymen, noticed anything amiss until the train left the track.

Evan Cameron, an Assistant Carriage Superintendent, examined the passenger vehicles at four in the afternoon and he found no broken springs, worn tyres or wheels out of gauge and he was able to state that all of the vehicles had been in the shops during the previous twelve months. He also explained that four fifths of the train was fitted with brakes which came on automatically when the first and second vehicles parted. James Woodhead, Outdoor Locomotive Superintendent, found the locomotive wheels to be equally true to gauge and with good tyres, and he went on to say that the driver, McKenley, was a particularly steady man who had known the line as driver and fireman since it opened seventeen years before.

Evidence was then given that although the track needed attention from time to time, this was not more so than on other lines. The sleepers had all been renewed since the line opened but the track needed occasional packing at this spot as the ground was rather soft. There had been a slip on the same bank, but nearer to Mayfield, during the previous winter and as there was a lot of chalk in the bank much rocky material had been brought down from Mayfield and put into it from time to time. Also, the inspector and the ganger had been given instructions to pay special attention to the permanent way at the bottom of the incline. At the time of the accident the line was under repair and one member of the repair gang was Stephen Holmwood, an uncle of the fireman, Minns. Another ganger had found pieces of the engine's brake gear by the track and he had shown them to Holmwood who visited his nephew in hospital a few days later. He was asked if anything had fallen off the engine but he replied that he did not know. In giving evidence Minns stated that he thought that the road had gone under the engine and he was probably right, the brake gear having been ripped off by the derailment. The track was not really in good condition and several drivers complained of it at the inquiry remarking that the outside rail often felt as if it had 'gone down'. It was a delicate position for Minns and Holmwood for they were each naturally anxious to avoid passing blame on the other.

Minns also gave evidence that they were coming down the bank at their normal speed of about forty miles an hour and he thought the driver applied the brakes to steady the train. The regulator was nearly closed when they went over and he remembered little more until he climbed out and a gentleman told him to close the regulator and draw the fire. Although in great pain, he managed to do so and he was warmly commended by Lt. Col. G. W. Addison, R.E., who was conducting the enquiry. Colonel Addison's conclusions were that the speed of the train had contributed to the cause of the accident together with the fact that the elevation of the outside rail of the curve was only half an inch instead of the desired two and a half inches. This may have been caused by the passage of the train but was more likely due to the heavy rain of the previous few days. In any case the defects in the line were largely due to its original course and these could only be removed by large alterations at great expense. Of more immediate interest was the guarding against a similar mishap on the line as it existed and if settlement was still to be expected on 'Tooth Bank' it would be necessary to reduce speed accordingly. Colonel Addison recommended that two extra minutes should be allowed, in both directions, between Heathfield and Mayfield and one minute extra between Heathfield and Horeham Road and between Mayfield and Rotherfield. Caution boards should be erected about two hundred and fifty yards on either side of the spot where the run off occurred and any attempt to save time be 'put a stop to at once'.[1]

Slips of earth from embankments had been a problem and reference has already been made to the severe slip which occurred near Mayfield shortly after the line opened. There was another extensive slip in December 1882 from a high embankment near Horeham Road which caused a discontinuance of passenger trains beyond Hailsham for more than three weeks and the *East Sussex News* reported that, in that time:

'a staff of upwards of 100 hands have been industriously engaged in repairing the embankment, the altitude of which, at some points is something like 80 feet. Sixty or seventy train loads of earth have been used to repair and strengthen the place where the slip occured.'[2]

The story of an amusing but potentially dangerous incident has already been published but it is well worth repeating here. On 17th December 1884 a late night train was about to leave Heathfield when Major Edwards, a wealthy landowner of Groombridge, ran on to the platform just as the guard was signalling the 'right away'. He was hurriedly assisted into a first class compartment before the staff noticed that he was very drunk. At Mayfield the Major complained bitterly of not having a ticket and on being supplied with one he held up the train while he visited the station toilet. On returning to his compartment the guard wisely locked both doors and no further thought was given to the matter until, between Rotherfield and Eridge, the Major suddenly appeared on the locomotive footplate complaining that a large dog had chased him out of the carriage window. With quick understanding the fireman pretended to drive off the dog with his shovel and the driver made their guest as comfortable

as possible on their coats so that he fell asleep. A hasty inspection of the train at Eridge showed that the compartment had indeed been left through the window and the passage to the engine made along the running boards of two carriages, a feat no sober man would have even contemplated. Needless to say, no fierce dog was discovered and the guard, station master and driver all agreed that the footplate was the safest place until Groombridge and the train set off. At Groombridge the Major refused to wake up and had to be taken on to Tunbridge Wells where a stop was made at a signal some four hundred yards before the platform. Coming to life quite suddenly, the unwanted guest threw off the coats and flung himself off the engine shouting 'Groombridge, Groombridge, all change'. All was then quiet and, as the signal cleared, the train was taken into the station where a search party with lanterns was organised. At the spot where the Major left the train there was a stream, swollen with flood water, at the foot of a steep embankment down which various marks showed his hurried descent. No body could be found so the course of the stream was followed until it passed into a culvert under the railway line. The search was then abandoned for it was considered that no human being could possible survive such a raging torrent. On return to the station a messenger was sent to call the police and the business of stabling the train and the engine began. The guard was writing his report in the station master's office when the police arrived and as the story was being told the young and very inexperienced booking clerk called for assistance saying 'a drunken tramp won't believe that the last train has left for Groombridge and he keeps beating off a huge dog that I can't see'. There was a rush for the ticket office where stood the missing Major Edwards, covered in mud, very wet, still very drunk, but very much alive. After the provision of dry clothing and black coffee he was sent home by special train. Later, on learning that the company was penalising the men concerned, he paid their fines and sent a cheque for £25 to the widows and orphans fund.[3]

[1]   Accident Report of G. W. Addison, Lt. Col. R.E., Assistant Secretary to the Board of Trade Railway Department, dated 31st October 1897.
[2]   East Sussex News: 12th January 1883.
[3]   Bradley, D. L. Locomotives of the LBSCR, Part 2, page 12.

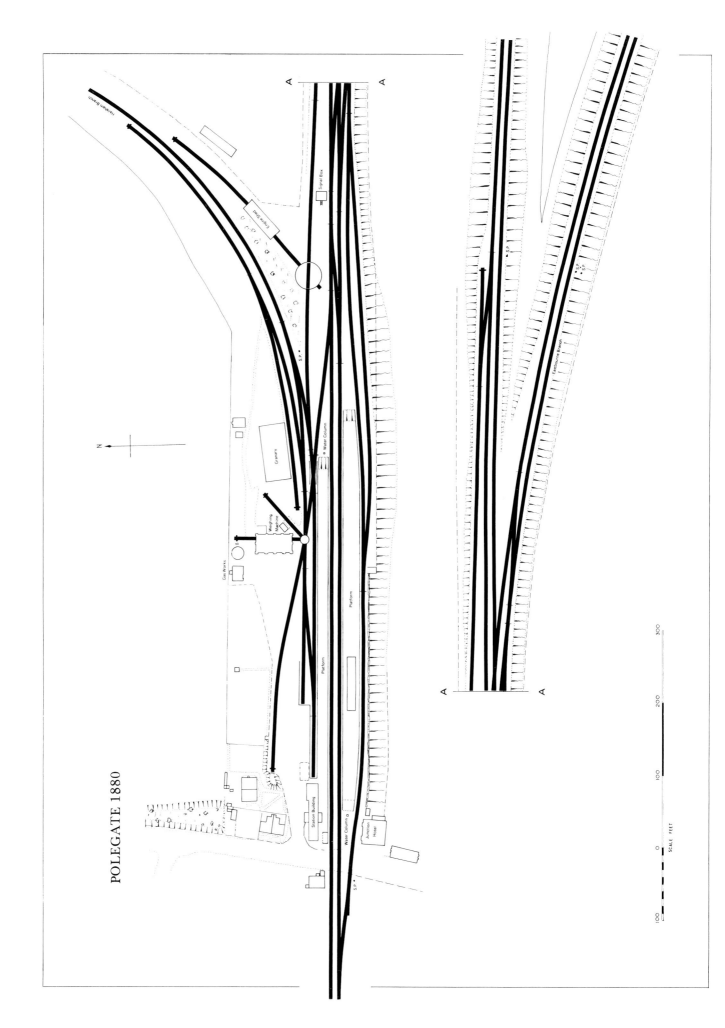

POLEGATE 1880

Hailsham Branch

Engine Shed

Signal Box

Granary

Gas Works

Weighing Machine

Water Column

Platform

Platform

Station Building

Water Column

Junction Hotel

S.P.

S.P.

Eastbourne Branch

S.P.

S.P.

S.P.

N

A A

A A

SCALE FEET

100 0 100 200 300

CHAPTER FIVE

STATIONS AND JUNCTIONS

POLEGATE

Two 1930s views showing the London end of Polegate station. The Cuckoo line branched off behind the goods yard.

O. J. Morris, cty. E. Jackson and Lens of Sutton

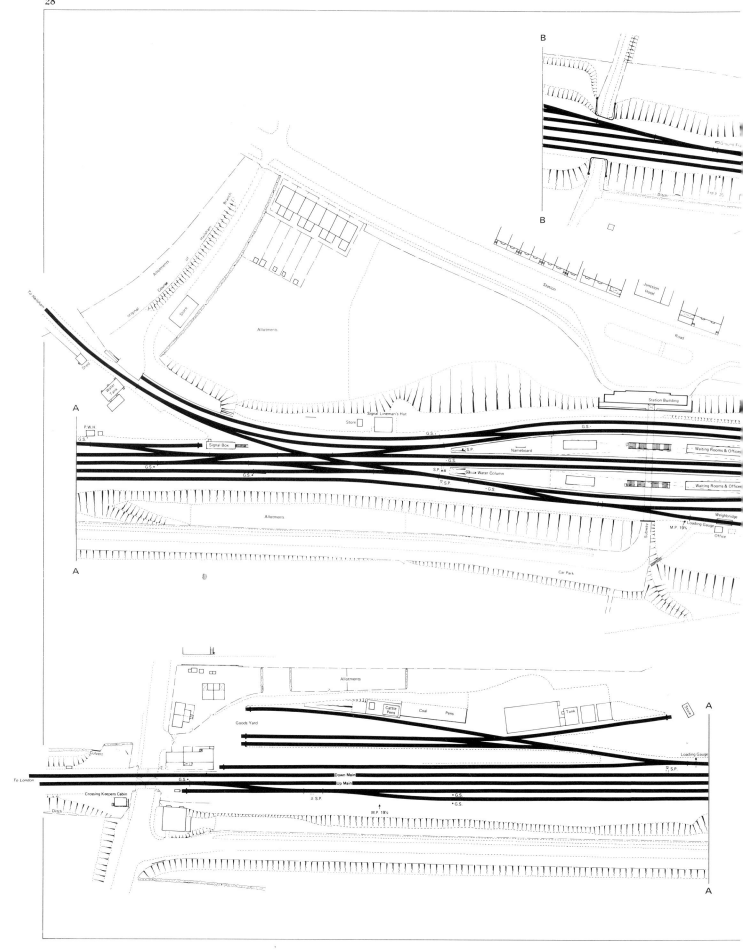

B

B

B

To Hailsham

Branch

of

Allotments

Course

original

Store

Allotments

Station

Junction
Hotel

Road

G'round Fr

Ditch

M.P 20

Station Building

A

Signal Lineman's Hut

Store

G.S.

G.S.

Water
Tank

Shed

P.W.H

G.S.

Signal Box

S.P

Nameboard

Waiting Rooms & Offices

G.S.

G.S.

S.P

Water Column

Waiting Rooms & Offices

S.P

G.S.

Allotments

Weighbridge

Subway

Loading Gauge

M.P. 19¾

Office

A

A

Car Park

Allotments

Goods Yard

Cattle
Pens

Coal

Pens

Tank

A

Culvert

Loading Gauge

S.P.

To London

Down Main

Up Main

G.S.

Crossing Keepers Cabin

S.P.

G.S.

Ditch

M.P. 19½

G.S.

A

A

POLEGATE 1961

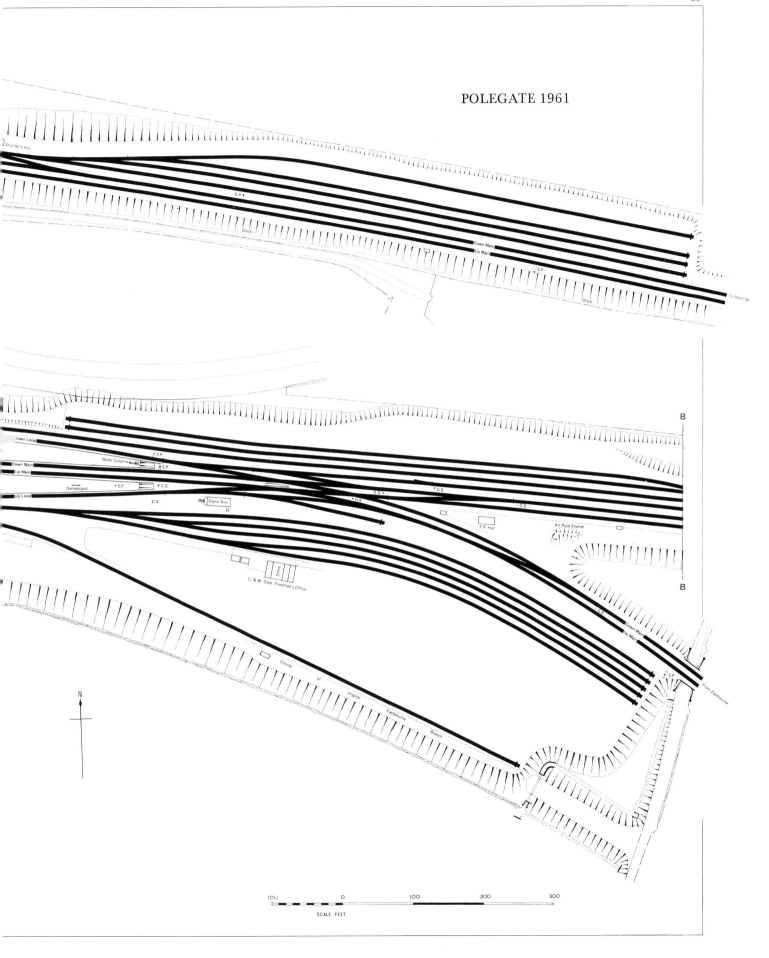

Shunter's Hut

S.P. •

Ditch

Down Main
Up Main

S.P.

Ditch

To Hastings

B

Down Loop

Down Main
Up Main

Water Column   • S.P.
                      • S.P.

Nameboard   • S.P.   • G.S.

Up Loop

Signal Box

G.S.   • G.S.
      • G.S.
                      • G.S.

T.P. Hut   Air Raid Shelter

C. & W. Dept. Foreman's Office   Store

B

• G.S.

Down Main
Up Main

N

Course   of   original   Eastbourne   Branch

• S.P.

From Eastbourne

• S.P.

S. C. Nash

Ex-LBSCR 'K' class 2—6—0 No. 32351 between Polegate and Hailsham on 12th June 1962.

'A1X' class 0—6—0 tank No. 32636 with the 5.34 p.m. Polegate to Hailsham train on 1st August 1952.   *S. C. Nash*

Re-built 'West Country' No. 34027 *Taw Valley* on the 8.44 a.m. Hailsham to Eastbourne train, approaching Polegate on 31st May 1963. For some years this was a regular 'filling-in' turn for a Bulleid Pacific.   *S. C. Nash*

HAILSHAM c.1874

Terminus Hotel

George Street

Cottages

School

Granary

Granary

Goods Shed

Platform

Station Building

Engine Shed

Kiln

Brickfield

N

Signal Box

Footpath

Subway

From Polegate

SCALE FEET

100   0   100   200   300

This view of Hailsham station and approach road, about 1869 or earlier, provides a rare view of the locomotive shed which was largely demolished during the early part of 1892. From this viewpoint the stone wall obscures the fence which is evident in the illustration which follows.

Hailsham Historical & Natural History Society

HAILSHAM

Until it was linked with Eridge in 1880, Hailsham was the terminus for a short branch from Polegate which opened on 14th May 1849 simultaneously with the branch from Polegate to Eastbourne. The original track layout at Polegate did not allow a direct through service between Hailsham and Eastbourne but, to a great extent, both branches were worked as one by a shuttle service which reversed direction at Polegate. This inconvenient arrangement continued for over thirty years until 3rd October 1881, thirteen months after the opening of the line through to Tunbridge Wells.

A single platform was sufficient for Hailsham while it was a terminus and a small station building contained the usual offices and other facilities. This was built of brown brick with red brick surrounds to the doors and windows and the roof was of tiles. However, the building does not seem to have conformed to any particular style as did those which were provided for the new lines of the 1860s and 1880s. Originally there was an ornamental tower with a steeple roof over the centre of the building and it has been suggested that this roof was of shingles. A popular feature in this part of Sussex, shingles were thin slates of oak which were cleft rather than sawn. When new they were a sort of corn yellow colour which quickly weathered to a silvery grey. The tower still existed in 1880, but it is

thought to have been removed during the following decade, possibly in 1884 when a Mr. Winter successfully tendered to repair and renovate the building for £84 15s 0d.[1]

The building might well have been a total loss in 1879 when a fire started in the lamp room, but prompt action by the station staff prevented serious damage[2] and, apart from the loss of its tower, the building remained virtually unaltered until it was demolished a few years after the station closed in 1969. The original canopy over the platform extended over the length of the building only and, with no valance, was similar in appearance to the canopy over the entrance which appears to have survived unaltered right to the end.

Reference to the track plans of 1875 and 1910, however, show that this building was about all that did survive from the original station and, although such alteration was immediately necessary for its use as a through station, many of the developments came in the following years. The original platform was on the 'down' side and a second platform, connected by a subway, was provided for the 'up' direction, but it is not clear whether any accommodation was provided on this platform to begin with. In December 1894, tenders were invited for the provision of waiting rooms and lavatories on the 'up' platform and plans for these were submitted in 1895.[3] These plans included the canopy and style of valance shown in the illustrations, and it is possible that the canopy on the 'down' platform was altered at the same time.

In 1890 a new porters' & lamp room and a coal store were built between the station building and the locomotive shed.[4] The existing lamp room was converted for use as the station master's office and store room.

The small locomotive shed shown on the plan of 1875 dates from 1858 but it fell into disuse after the extension of the branch in 1880. When a new house for the station master was authorised in December 1891, the estimated cost at £275 allowed for the re-use of materials to be salvaged from the shed and a schoolroom which were due for demolition.[5] The new house was evidently completed by the middle of the following year as the half-yearly report of June 1892 shows the account to have been settled. One wall of the locomotive shed survived, however, to support the extended canopy over the 'down' platform. An extensive cattle dock and cattle pens developed in the area formerly occupied by the shed and reference has already been made to the special arrangements for cattle traffic on Hailsham cattle market days. At the northern end of the station, and also on the 'down' side, there were side and end loading facilities for horse-boxes, prize cattle vans and road vehicles.

The large goods warehouse, shown on the later plans, replaced the small shed in 1888 and is an indication of the growing freight traffic, as also is the considerable enlargement of the goods yard. The warehouse was equipped with a thirty hundredweight crane and a larger five ton crane stood in the yard. As well as general sidings, there was a

By the time this photograph was taken there had been some considerable growth of the trees and bushes, telegraph poles have appeared on the scene and the locomotive shed has been provided with smoke vents.   *Hailsham Historical & Natural History Society*

coal yard where the privately owned wagons of the coal merchants, White & Beeny, and George Harmer & Co., could be seen from early days up to about 1939. Originally White and Beeny were separate firms who appear in local directories of the 1850s. Mr. White ran a grocery, wine and spirit business while William Beeny was the local coal merchant. By 1868 Beeny had expanded his business by opening a branch at Eastbourne[5] and, according to an

One of the trains which provided the shuttle service to Polegate and Eastbourne stands at the platform in the days when Hailsham was a terminus. The crossover seen here does not feature on the plan of 1874.   *Hailsham Historical & Natural History Society*

The line has been extended to Tunbridge Wells, but, as the station master's house has not yet been built, the date of this illustration is between 1880 and 1892. The brake-third carriage appears to be of 1863 vintage. *Hailsham Historical & Natural History Society*

advertisement in the *East Sussex News*, by 1871 he was using his own wagons.

W. BEENY, HAILSHAM
DELIVERS COAL of ALL DESCRIPTIONS
in his OWN TRUCKS, to ANY STATION, London,
Brighton, and South-Coast, and Tunbridge Wells and Hastings
Railways, at moderate prices.[7]

Both White and Beeny had sons who joined their fathers in business, both firms having '& Sons' added to their titles by the 1880s. About 1890 William Beeny's two sons took over the business, one taking Hailsham and the other, Arthur John Beeny, taking Eastbourne. The latter continued to trade until the 1930s but the former, or possibly his son, joined with one of White's descendants to form White and Beeny. George Harmer and Company were in business at Hailsham from 1885 until 1949 when the firm moved to Suffolk. Their wagons, built between 1902 and 1912, were in a livery of red-oxide with white lettering shaded with black. The firm also owned motor lorries which were painted red and chocolate-brown.

Over on the 'down' side, and south of the cattle pens, was a private siding to a brickworks. This dated from an agreement of 1919 between the railway company and the owners, Messrs. Burtenshaw & Green, which was sealed in 1921.[8] This siding was entered from the 'down' siding,

through points operated by a simple throw-over lever, and protected by a gate, the key of which was held in the signal box. No movement was allowed on this siding once a train had left Waldron for Hailsham unless the facing points in the 'down' line were set for the single line.[9] During the early 1920s Burtenshaw & Green received and despatched an average of five wagons daily, but no evidence has been found to suggest that the company ever owned any rail vehicles.

Another private siding situated on the 'up' side about half-way between Hailsham and Polegate, served the Eastbourne House Land and Trading Company under an agreement of 1899. When this company later ceased trading the siding became derelict, but in 1921 the Polegate Brick and Tile Company were authorised to take it over and repair it for their own use under the same terms as the previous agreement of 1899.[10] All traffic for this siding was required to circulate through Hailsham and the key to the gate was obtained from Hailsham signal box, but returned to Polegate signal box.[11]

Although the ground frame was still in position in 1950 the siding was no longer connected and again in a derelict condition.

In 1880 the first of the new style of signal boxes were provided at Hailsham. With red brick bases and timber

By the beginning of this century the approach road to the station had been provided with a pavement although the road itself was still in a rough state. All that remains of the locomotive shed is the west wall which supports the canopy over the platform. *Lens of Sutton*

The view south from the road bridge at the northern end of the station. The station master's house, built in 1892, is to the left of the picture. The train standing at the 'up' platform is probably one of the shuttle service trains waiting to return to Eastbourne for this platform was signalled for departures in both directions. *Lens of Sutton*

A view similar to the last illustration but at a later date, thought to be between 1905 and 1910. The train standing at the 'down' platform appears to consist of Stroudley's four-wheeled stock and the passenger cattle van at the carriage dock is one of twenty-three built in 1892. The legend 'Eridge' is chalked on the side in the second panel from the left. The point rodding has lost most of the board walk shown in the previous view.

Lens of Sutton

Looking north during the 'thirties. The surviving wall of the locomotive shed supports the canopy over the 'down' platform. Whilst the point and signal rodding has again been covered with a board walk, later illustrations show that it was yet again removed. The rodding no longer runs right through the station. *Lens of Sutton*

upperworks, they were similar to those provided at each of the five new stations, the only apparent differences being in the positioning of the doors and stairway. There were also variations in the dimensions. The large box at Hailsham, on the 'down' side at the southern end of the station, was 17 ft 6 ins long by 11 ft 6 ins wide with a floor height of 8 ft. The small box, set into the 'up' platform at the Northern

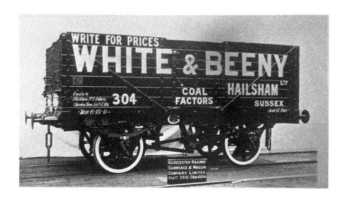

One of the wagons of the Hailsham Coal Merchants, White & Beeney, as photographed by the GRC & W Co. in 1931. The small lettering reads 'Empty to: Markham No. 2 Colliery, Town, L. & N.E. Rly.' A. G. Thomas gives the livery as black with white lettering shaded green. *GRC & W Co.*

end, was 13 ft 6 ins long by 9 ft 6 ins wide with a floor height of 4 ft 8 ins above ground level.

After 1880 Hailsham continued to be used as the terminus for the shuttle service from Polegate and Eastbourne and the 'up' platform was also signalled for departures in the 'down' direction. During every period covered by the timetables quoted there were more departures from Hailsham than arrivals, but the timetables do not make it clear how these workings were balanced. Some of the shuttle services were worked by motor trains, but others were worked by main line locomotives filling in between other turns. In modern times it was not uncommon to see a 'Bulleid Pacific' at the head of a one or two coach train. During most of its existence Hailsham handled over thirty passenger train arrivals and departures each weekday as well as four goods arrivals and departures.

[1] Engineering Committee Meeting: 21.5.1884 Minute 2.
[2] *Sussex Express*: 1.2.1879.
[3] Drawing held by C.C.E. Southern Region.
[4] Engineering Committee Meeting: 29.7.1880 Minute 2.
[5] Engineering Committee Meeting: 1.12.1891 Minute 9.
[6] *East Sussex News* (Advertisement) 24.1.1868.
[7]   ,,   ,,   ,,   ,,   6.10.1871.
[8] Engineering Committee Meeting: 5.1 10 919 Minute 7
     ,,   ,,   ,,   2.2.1921 Minute 10.
[9] Appendix to the Working Timetable 1921.
[10] Engineering Committee Meeting: 19.1.1921 Minute 21.
[11] Appendix to the Working Timetable 1921.

38

From Polegate

A

A

A

A

Coal Pens

Tank

Footpath

Pipe

M.P. 22¾

Loading Gauge

S.P.

S.P.

Subway

Signal Box

N

From Polegate

C

C

M.P. 22

Whistle Board

Burtenshaw & Green's Siding

Brickworks

C

C

Allotments

Allotments

Allotments

9" Pipe

Signal Gantry

Loading Gauge

G.S.

M.P. 22¾

G.S.

Subway

Signal Box

S.P.

Coal

Retaining

100   0   100   200   300

SCALE FEET

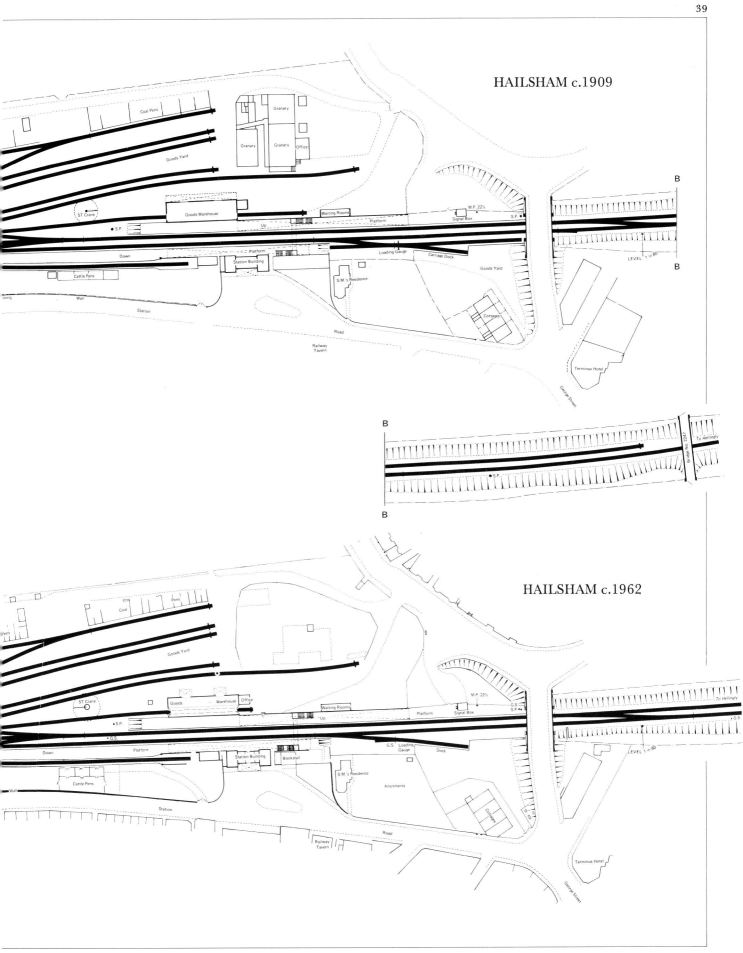

HAILSHAM c.1909

HAILSHAM c.1962

Hailsham station from the south on 11th June 1965. The cattle pens may be seen beyond the 'down' starting signal. Although the goods yard is becoming overgrown, it is still in use and a 'Scammel' trailer is backed up to the warehouse. *John Scrace*

Originally one long canopy extended over the whole length of the forecourt side of the goods warehouse at Hailsham. *Author*

The large signal box at the southern end of Hailsham. *John Scrace*

'I.1X' class 4—4—2 tank No. 2005, having run round its one-coach train, is waiting to return to Eastbourne. Four of this class, Nos. 2005, 2008, 2009 and 2010, were included in the Eastbourne allocation of 1946. Note that the siding accommodation at the end-loading dock has been reduced by this time.
Lens of Sutton

Eleven months after closure the station begins to look derelict, but this illustration does show details of the framework of the timber screen wall of the 'down' platform.
Author

Although the siding to the end loading dock survives, the facilities appear to have been out of use for some time when this photograph was taken about 1950.
Collection John Minnis

'I.3' class No. 32022 about to depart from Hailsham with an 'up' train c.1950.
Collection John Minnis

No. 32325 with the 9.55 a.m. train from Eastbourne to Tunbridge Wells waiting at Hailsham for 'E.5' class 0–6–2 tank No. 32405 with the 9.08 a.m. train from Tunbridge Wells to clear the single line from Horam.   *S. C. Nash*

Hellingly from the air in 1959. There is little activity in the goods yard but the coal merchant appears to be thriving. The line to the hospital is clearly visible curving away to the right.

R. G. Spalding

A northbound train arriving at Hellingly in the period soon after the opening of the line to the hospital. This is obviously not one of the connecting services for the hospital for the chains are up on the hospital platform. No photographer ever seems to have been present when the hospital tramcar was in use. In the original drawings of the station the lavatories are shown at the other end of the building as at Mayfield and Rotherfield. The plans for the alteration of 1905 show these already in existence at the near end as in this picture. The early photograph of Waldron, included later, shows a similar arrangement, suggesting that the original plans were not followed. *Lens of Sutton*

HELLINGLY

The casual visitor to Hellingly might well gain a misleading impression, but the village certainly appears to have success-fully resisted many of the influences of the past century. Two main roads avoid the village, and for eighty-five years the railway passed within a few hundred yards of it, and yet it was possible to travel by either method and still be unaware of the group of tile-hung cottages around the oval shaped churchyard with its twelfth century church. The churchyard is on a mound which is believed to be a Saxon burial ground and the only one in the country to survive intact. When the railway was opened in 1880 the station was about three hundred and fifty yards from the village, but neither seems to have had much effect upon the other. Indeed, the level of facilities originally provided at the station suggests that the railway company had little expec-tation of any significant or immediate increase in traffic. It was a first appointment for the station master, a Mr. Pilbeam, who had been a clerk at Littlehampton, and he was responsible for a single line of track serving one platform, and an extensive plot of grass land which 'had been secured here for a goods yard, as the traffic dev-eloped'[1] Evidently the traffic did develop in due course for two sidings were laid and the yard was opened for use in 1890.[2] However, the real development at Hellingly came from what must have been a totally unexpected source, the construction of an asylum nearby.

The first of the new style of station building was at Hellingly and, although much modified, it still survives as a private residence to the present day. In common with all of the other new stations, it was built in the Tudor style, but renovation of the building was required in 1891 and it is probable that this was when the Tudor effect was hidden by weather tiling.[3] At the northern end of the platform was one of the small signal boxes and this was in use until 15th February 1930, when it was replaced by a ground frame. The box was provided for the opening of the line, despite the fact that the station was in the middle of a block section and there was no passing loop, no signals and no points to operate until 1890, when the goods yard was brought into use. It was on 2nd February of that year that Major General Hutchinson, of the Board of Trade, reported on the new connection for the goods yard at Hellingly and sanctioned the use thereof. To begin with, the facilities were limited to the two sidings which could be served only by trains travelling in the 'down' direction, but in July 1890 the provision of coal wharves and approaches was authorised at an estimated cost of £63.[4] There are also references to a new goods shed in the Half-Yearly Reports for December 1899 and June 1890, when payments of £637 and £185 7s 2d are shown in the respective accounts. This is curious for, quite apart from the unlikely sum of money involved, no shed of the size indicated was erected at the time, and three years later it was considered necessary to provide a lock-up goods shed at an estimated cost of £60.[5] A large warehouse is shown, however, on the 1910 plan and some of the illustrations.

The two existing sidings were lengthened during 1898[6] and a third siding was added during the following year. This was probably in readiness for the traffic to be generated by

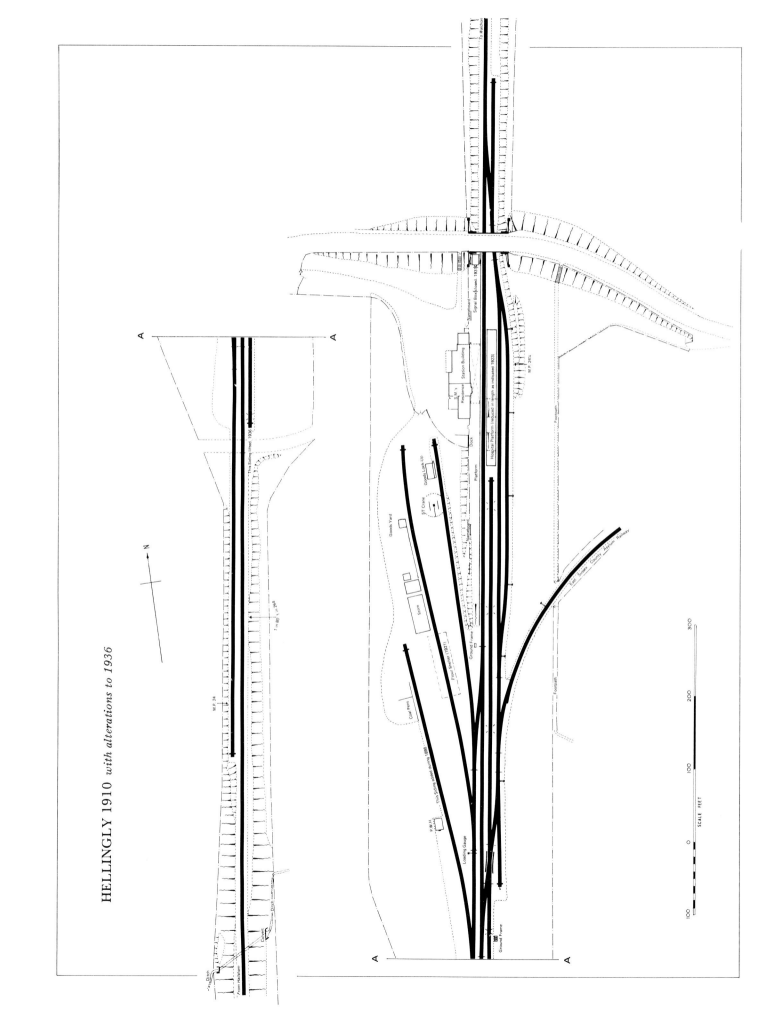

HELLINGLY 1910 *with alterations to 1936*

Hellingly Station : L. B. & S. C.

A train arriving at Hellingly from the Tunbridge Wells direction soon after the opening of the line to the hospital. The hospital platform was protected by chains which were removed when connections with the hospital tramcar were due. The small signal box may be seen behind the locomotive. *Lens of Sutton*

the construction of the new lunatic asylum, as it was then called, about a mile to the east of the station. In October of 1899 a private siding from Hellingly goods yard to the site was authorised, subject to the East Sussex County Council providing the payment of the entire cost which was estimated at £1,700.[7] The siding, which was a little over a mile in length, was constructed by the contractors for the building of the asylum, stores and material being conveyed to the site, until the asylum was completed, by the contracror's own steam locomotive. Before permitting the use of the siding, the Board of Trade suggested moving the signal box to the south of the station but agreed with the railway company when they said that the small amount of traffic would not justify the cost. Sanction was given on 5th July 1900.

On the completion of the asylum in 1905, the line was electrified and taken over by the East Sussex County Council to provide transport for patients, staff and visitors and to carry coal and provisions. In readiness for this, an application was made during the previous year by the County Council to the railway company 'for the provision of a separate platform for the use of patients for the County Asylum and to keep them apart from the ordinary passengers.' It was agreed that the platform should be constructed at an estimated cost of £500 to the Council.[8] At the same time a loop and sidings with shunting spurs were provided for the interchange of goods traffic. The siding was single track with two intermediate loop sidings and for about half its length it was within the hospital grounds. Electric current was supplied by the overhead system at 500 volts DC and this was generated by the hospital's own plant which was also connected to the National Grid. All the points on the line, including the connections at Hellingly, were hand-operated and there were no signals. The key to the gate protecting the line was held by the hospital authorities and a catchpoint was provided just outside the gate.

After leaving the main line, the hospital railway passed through the gate from the station yard and after a short distance crossed two roads in quick succession, neither of which were protected by level crossing gates. A little beyond the second crossing came the first of the loops which was known as Farm Siding and was once used for loading agricultural produce for the hospital. Half-way from Hellingly, where there was another loop siding, the line

Although the passenger service to the hospital had been discontinued for two years when this photograph was taken on 10th October 1933, the hospital platform was still in existence. It had been reduced in length in 1922. The siding to the end of the platform was removed in 1936. The signal box had also gone by 1933. *H. C. Casserley*

entered the hospital grounds and ran parallel with a tree-lined avenue for about half a mile before curving round into the hospital power station. On the curve there was a loop with a short siding into the workshop and at the beginning of the curve there was an 'Avery' twenty-ton wagon weighbridge. Another siding, just before the weighbridge, ran to a platform for passengers.

Two pieces of motive power were provided, a four-wheeled steeple-cab locomotive for goods traffic and an odd-looking four-wheeled tramcar. The locomotive was quite a curiosity in its own right for, although it carried the builder's plates of both R. Blackwell and Company Limited and W. Whitely and Son Limited, neither firm admits to any knowledge of it. The control equipment was of German manufacture and the locomotive may have been also, but all dimensions were in imperial rather than metric units. A headlamp was mounted at one end only and there was an electric bell on the cab bulkhead at the other end. The one fourteen horse-power motor with a 6½ to 1 gear ratio was nose-mounted at the headlamp end of the frame and was just capable of coping with two loaded twelve-ton coal wagons up the one in fifty gradient to the hospital. The tram car type controller was at the headlamp end of the cab and the horizontal hand-brake wheel was mounted in one

Some thirty-five years later the main changes include the absence of the hospital platform and the addition of the flour shelter which may be seen just beyond the canopy.

Collection John Minnis

corner. The switch gear and contact breakers were fully exposed immediately above the controller and between the cab windows. The single trolley pole was of the tramcar type and mounted centrally on the cab roof. Couplings were of the three link variety. The locomotive was painted a dark green in its later years, but it was probably dark red like the tramcar, when first built.

The tramcar was a curious little vehicle with its interior fitted out in light oak and shaped plywood panelled seating

for twelve, six on each side, in two small saloons. It was originally dark red with yellow lining and red wheels but this was later changed to dark green. There was no builder's plate on the car but it was almost certainly constructed by the Brush Engineering Company for the wheels carried the inscription 'British Barrow Griffin Company, mfd. for Brush Co. Jan 25 1904' and the body was similar in design to coaches previously built by the Falcon Company for the Corris Railway in Wales. The single electric motor was

A train approaching from the Tunbridge Wells direction in 1939. The hospital platform has been removed by this time but the line to the hospital was still used for goods traffic.

Lens of Sutton

On 22nd May 1954 the Southern Counties Touring Society arranged a 'Special' over the line to the hospital. The train, consisting of the electric locomotive and a British Railways brake van, is shown waiting at Hellingly station. *J. H. Meredith*

Hellingly from the south, showing the line to the hospital on the right and part of the goods yard on the left. The 'flour' shelter is very evident.

Collection John Minnis

On 4th April 1959, shortly before the closure of the line, a final 'Special' was arranged for the Norbury Transport and Model Railway Club. This view shows the beautiful route through the hospital grounds. *A. E. Bennett*

The Hellingly Hospital rolling stock consisted of a weed-killing tank wagon and a coal wagon. The latter was built on the frame and wheels of the old tramcar. *J. H. Meredith*

The hospital-owned electric locomotive at Hellingly station on 19th September 1953.

S. C. Nash

Mr. Greenwood, the engineer, with the locomotive driver on 28th October 1950.   *J. H. Meredith*

The 1954 'Special' at the hospital end of the line.   *J. H. Meredith*

wound on one axle and there were, presumably, controllers at each end, although the actual platform shape and fittings can only be surmised for both have long since disappeared. Current collection was almost certainly by trolley pole similar to that on the locomotive.

The tramcar service connected with the 'main line' trains at Hellingly but there was no timetable for goods traffic which depended upon requirements. When loaded wagons for the hospital arrived at Hellingly the station master informed the hospital authorities who arranged for their collection. The locomotive from the hospital was accompanied by a shunter who, in addition to his normal duties, flagged trains over the level crossings and opened the gates at the station yard. An average of six wagons a day in winter and four wagons a day in summer were handled for the hospital during the 1920s period.[9]

By the end of 1904 it was found that the waiting room accommodation was insufficient at the station, 'particularly on days when the County Asylum is open to visitors', and it was ordered that the improvements indicated on plans submitted to the railway company should be carried out at an estimated cost of £350.[10] It will be seen from the illustration and the drawings that these improvements completely altered the character of the building.

When the hospital passenger service was discontinued in 1931 the body of the tramcar was removed to the hospital sports field for use as a pavilion and it was still there some thirty years later. The underframe and axles were used in the construction of a five-ton low-sided wagon. The hospital also owned a ten-ton high-sided clinker wagon of LBSCR origin, built in 1888. Both of these wagons were used for internal movements of coal and coke. The hospital platform at Hellingly, which had already been reduced in

length in 1922, was removed altogether soon after 1933 and the passenger platform at the hospital end of the line came into use as a coal stage. The line to the hospital remained in use for goods traffic until 1959 when the locomotive was believed to be the oldest electric locomotive still operating in the British Isles. In that year, however, the hospital power station was converted to use fuel oil, which would be delivered by road tanker, and the line was closed completely. During its last ten years the hospital railway attracted the attention of several enthusiasts' societies and a number of 'specials' were arranged using a British Railways brake van for the passengers, hauled by the hospital locomotive.

In addition to the traffic generated by the hospital, regular quantities of flour were carried from Hellingly.

The tramcar body survived in a modified form as the hospital sports pavilion.   *J. H. Meredith*

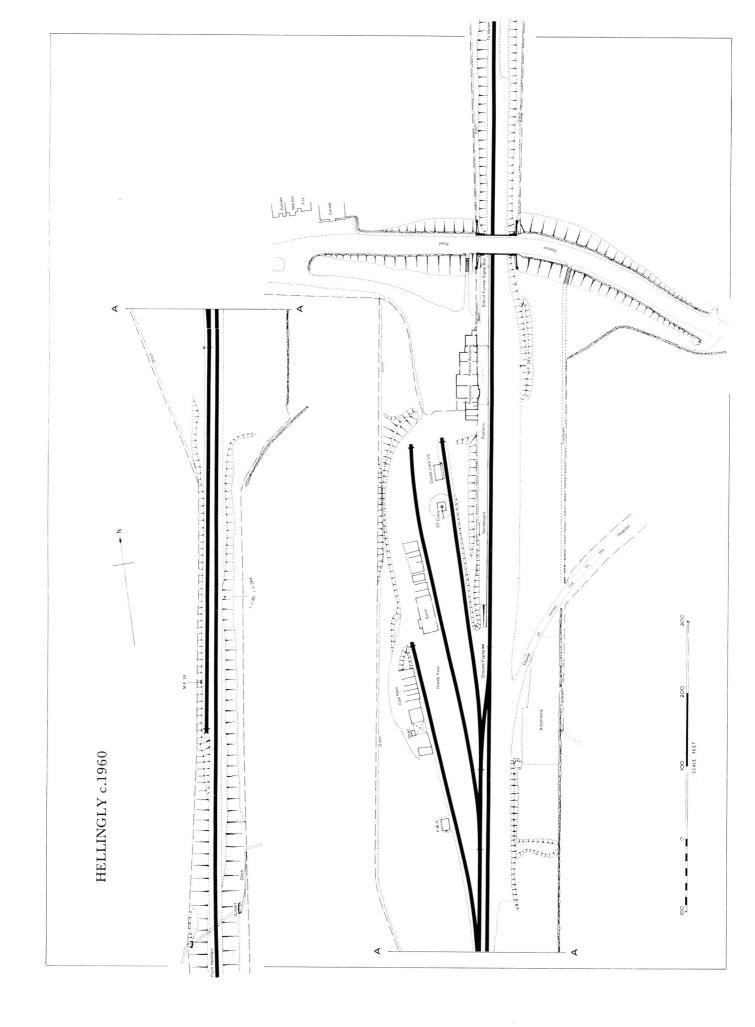

HELLINGLY c.1960

By the time this picture was taken on 24th May 1965, there was virtually no trace of all the additions of the early part of the century.

John Scrace

About half a mile to the south, at Horsebridge, there was a mill belonging to McDougall's who used rail transport until a road haulage firm won the contract early in the 1950s. By 1921, however, this traffic was sufficiently important to the railway company for them to provide a shelter over one of the sidings in order to give some protection when transhipping the products of the mill. The shelter was a very simple structure consisting of a tarred and felted roof supported on standards formed from old rails. It had been part of an existing shelter, which was no longer required, in Battersea goods yard. The estimated cost of this work was £145.[11]

During the second world war Park House, an annexe of the hospital, was used as a military hospital for the Canadian Army and according to local recollections it was not uncommon for ambulance trains to be seen at Hellingly station. The light construction of the hospital line would not permit them to proceed closer.

[1] *The Sussex Express*: 24.4.1880.
[2] Engineering Committee Meeting: 25.2.1890. Minute 2.
[3]   ,,   ,,   ,,   14.7.1891. Minute 5.
[4]   ,,   ,,   ,,   29.7.1890. Minute 2.
[5]   ,,   ,,   ,,   31.10.1893. Minute 4.
[6]   ,,   ,,   ,,   16.3.1898. Minute 7.
[7]   ,,   ,,   ,,   11.10.1899. Minute 7.
[8]   ,,   ,,   ,,   28.5.1902. Minute 12.
[9] *Railways*: April, 1951.
    Railway Magazine: December, 1957.
    Model Railway News: September 1960 & January 1961.
[10] Plans held by CCE (SR).
[11] Engineering Committee Meeting: 2.8.1922. Minute 3.

This illustration shows clearly the alternate bands of plain and decorative hung tiles used to cover the original 'Tudor' style.

Author

A north-bound train drawing into Waldron during the early part of this century. The pattern of tiles on the upper walls of the station master's house differed from that at Hellingly in that there were alternately four rows of plain tiles and three rows of decorative tiles.

Lens of Sutton

An early photograph of 'Waldron and Horeham Road' showing the original style of the five new stations on the line. The location of the gentlemen's toilet at the near end of the building is of interest for the original drawings show this at the far end of the building, as at Mayfield and Rotherfield.   *Hailsham Historical & Natural History Society*

HORAM

It would seem that both the LBSCR and its successor, the Southern Railway, found it difficult to settle upon an identity for this station and it has been suggested that the name gave the Victorian mind some cause for concern. The name comes from the village of Waldron, some two miles away, and Horeham Manor which was close by. To further confuse the issue, the next station up the line, Heathfield, was actually in the parish of Waldron and a newspaper item headed 'Lost Property'[1] expressed the hope that the station would not be called Waldron as it might be confounded with Waddon. Quite considerable development took place within the vicinity of the station, however, and it is this settlement which is now known as Horam. The development continued after the closure of the railway and it is now quite difficult to find the site of the station.

Mr. Breeds, formerly station master at West Brighton, was 'entrusted with the responsible task of organising the traffic and getting the station into working order.'[2] This could not have been an easy task for on 24th April 1880 it was reported that 'at present the waiting rooms are of timber, but both here and at Hellingly substantial buildings

of red brick, with stone facings, are in course of erection.'[2] The building, which was on the up platform, was virtually identical to the one at Hellingly before that building was enlarged to cater for the increased hospital traffic. The original Tudor appearance was lost during 1890 when repairs to and painting of the station buildings, including weather-tiling the exterior of the station master's residence, was authorised at an estimated cost of £149.[3] Access to the down platform was by the roadbridge, and wooden stairways were provided from the end of each platform up to road level. It may be seen from the plan of 1961, however, that the stairway to the down platform had gone and a wide path led down to a gate to the south of the waiting room where, it is understood, there was a second ticket office at this time. This waiting room was a small timber building with a tiled roof, and a canopy covered the platform in front of it. Originally the building was open to the platform but a door and screen were provided at an early date, possibly in 1891 when similar work was carried out at Barcombe Mills station on the Uckfield line.

Two signal boxes were provided for the opening of the line and the larger of these, Waldron South, contained 18 levers. Waldron North, the smaller box, was sited at the end of the up platform by the road bridge and, although it

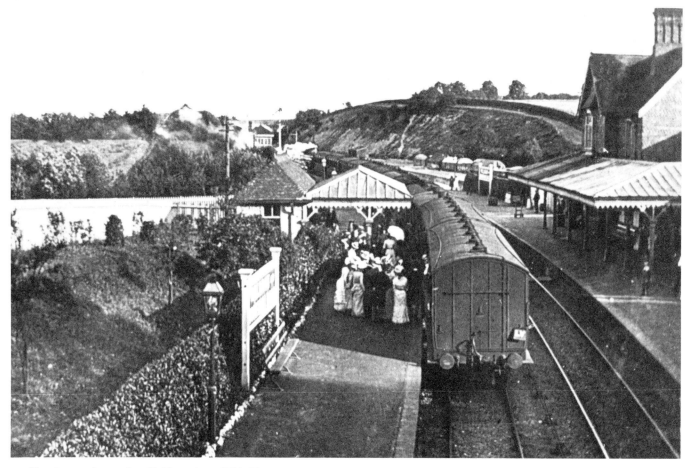

The view to the south at Waldron about 1900. The nameboard gives the station its post-1900 title. The 'down' starting signal is in the post-1897 style when a white stripe replaced a black stripe on the signal arm.
Lens of Sutton

is not shown on a large scale railway survey of 1889, various records, including those of Saxby and Farmer, confirm that it did date from 1880. Both boxes were in use until 30th March 1930, when the North box closed. On On 28th August 1935 Waldron South Box was also closed and an eighteen-lever frame was provided on the platform in front of the booking office where the block instruments were installed. Now known as Waldron, the frame was protected by an iron railing surround. During the 1950s the railings were replaced by a brick and timber structure as shown in the illustrations and on 21st September 1959 the box was renamed 'Horam'.

Goods facilities, which were very limited, consisted of three sidings, one of which served an end-loading dock. Neither a warehouse nor a crane of any kind was provided but in 1900 it was recommended that lock-up goods storage should be provided at an estimated cost of £95[4] and in April of that year a Mr. Watson contracted to erect such a store for £59 17s 0d.[5] Probably the most important item to be handled at this station was milk and, according to local recollections, farmers brought the milk in churns to the station where it was transferred to milk tank wagons. A special milktrain, scheduled to depart for Eastbourne at 8.20 p.m., was shown in the working timetable for July 1934, and reference has already been made in Chapter 3 to the collection of milk by the 8.20 p.m. down train from Heathfield. In due course the Express Dairy Company

An early view of Horam station building and approach. In common with Rotherfield, the entrance porch lost its leaded panes and decorative mouldings in later years.   *Author's Collection*

established a depot at Horam, and a siding to the depot was laid on the down side of the line during the late thirties. Again, from local recollections, milk tanks were attached to up trains and it was preferred to use London bound trains in order to avoid transfers at Eridge. It is thought that the depot was equipped with a ramp and a loading bank to allow the use of road tank vehicles on flat wagons. During the early 1950s a road haulage company were able

This aerial view of Horam in 1959 is of particular interest because it clearly shows the private siding to the Express Dairy Company. The goods yard has a collection of open wagons, most of which are empty. Coal traffic seems to have been the main source of revenue.

R. G. Spalding

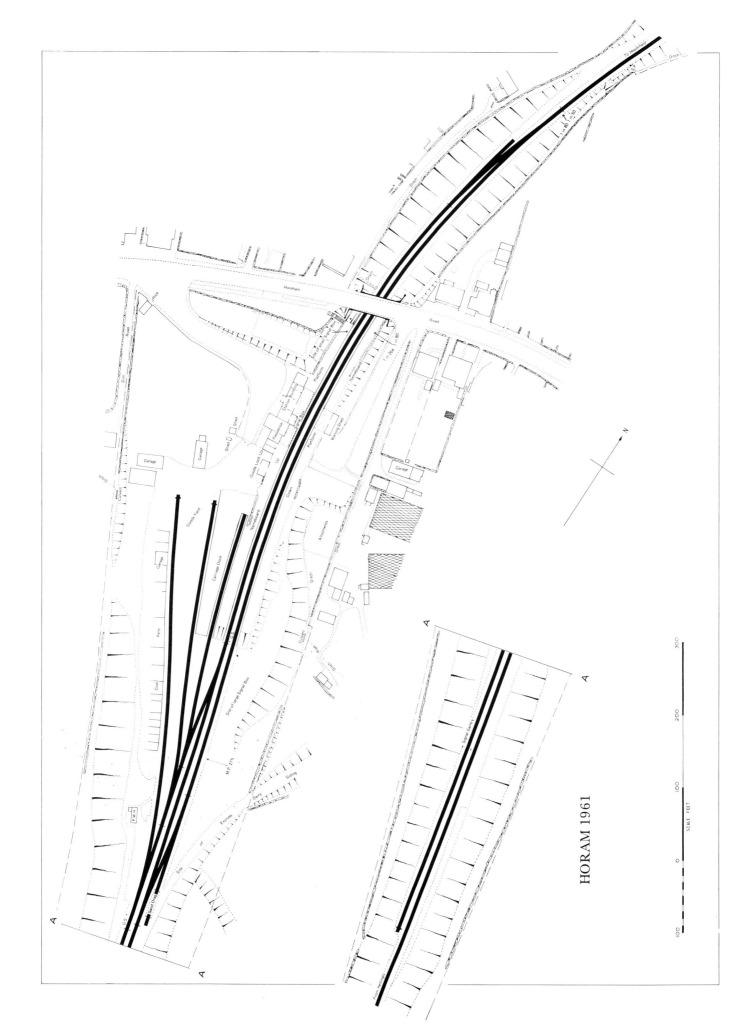

HORAM 1961

SCALE FEET

Above: No. 80089 at Horam with the 1.40 p.m. Heathfield to Eastbourne on 11th June 1965. *John Scrace*

Left: As a measure of economy during the 1930s, the duties of porter and signalman at Horam were combined. The small box at the end of the up platform was demolished and a lever frame was positioned in front of the ticket office. Originally, the frame was protected with iron railings, the brick surround shown here being provided some time after 1957. *Author*

to quote a slightly cheaper rate than the railway who then lost the contract. It was not an unusual story during that period. Oil traffic may also have provided revenue for the railway for a while for in 1915 authority was given for the Bowring Petroleum Company to build an oil depot at the station.[6] This was to be partly in the goods yard and partly on land rented from the railway company. Four years later authority was given for an additional oil tank to be erected.[7]

Horam station won the Southern Sales League competition of the Southern Railway in 1938 and a bronze shield to commemorate this was presented to Mr. Powell, the station master, by the general manager of the Southern Railway. This shield was awarded to the station showing the greatest proportional increase in takings for the year.[8]

[1] The *Sussex Express*: 7.2.1880.
[2] ,, ,, ,, 24.4.1880.
[3] Engineering Committee Meeting: 17.6.1890. Minute 4.
[4] ,, ,, ,, 28.2.1900. Minute 4.
[5] ,, ,, ,, 11.4.1900. Minute 2.
[6] ,, ,, ,, 6.10.1915. Minute 9.
[7] ,, ,, ,, 13.8.1919. Minute 3.
[8] The *Sussex Express*: 24.2.1939.

The lock-up goods shed at Waldron differed in detail from that at Hellingly. *Collection John Minnis*

'C2' class 0–6–0 No. 2436 was one of three surviving members of the class which had not been rebuilt to 'C2X'. It is seen here with the 2.45 p.m. goods from Tunbridge Wells to Polegate on 28th May 1949.
Collection John Scrace

'I3' class 4–4–2 tank No. 32029 entering Horam with the 10.42 a.m. Tunbridge Wells to Eastbourne train during 1949. When the new Eastern and Central Sections Engine Restriction Book was issued on 1st February 1937, this class was prohibited over all the single lines in East Sussex, including the Heathfield line. This restriction was relaxed in 1940, however, and during 1948 Eastbourne shed acquired several of the class for working this line until they were withdrawn in 1951. By the end of 1948 Eastbourne's allocation had become: 32030, 32077, 32081, 32083 and 32089.
S. C. Nash

The artists who coloured the early postcards tended to paint out certain background details and it cannot be certain, therefore, that the additional buildings shown in this illustration suggest a date later than the one overleaf. *Lens of Sutton*

HEATHFIELD

Heathfield is about halfway between Tunbridge Wells and Eastbourne and, because of its location perhaps, it has always had more importance than the other villages along the route. Whatever its relative importance before the railway came, however, there can be no doubt that the Heathfield district was more affected by the railway than any other part of the area.

The village was well established by the fourteenth century with the grant of a fair and a market in 1315 but the settlement dates from much earlier times. Although the Weald (wildwood) was originally covered with dense forest, it is thought that the ridges were only lightly wooded and formed routes, even for prehistoric man. Several of these routes met in the Heathfield area and settlements developed where the Saxons made clearances in the forests along the way. During the time of the Roman occupation, they were used as trade routes which eventually developed into the roads of today. Until more recent times, however, these roads were impassable in winter and up to the coming of the railway the villages were virtually cut off from each other in bad weather. The geological nature of the area provided poor farmland but oak trees flourished and a considerable amount of timber went to the royal dockyard at Chatham for ship building. The timber was transported by horse-drawn tugs, but it was not unknown for a consignment to take up to three years to reach its destination,

making progress during the summer months only. The farming which did develop specialised mostly in stock-rearing and dairying and there was a widespread cottage industry in chicken fattening. Other crafts included brick and tile making, charcoal burning, tanning, wheel-wrighting and, of course, mining for the iron industry which was at its height from the fifteenth to the eighteenth century.

The new ease of travel and transport of bulk materials which came with the railway changed the outlook of Heathfield with a shift away from the land and a growth of commerce. The railway brought prosperity but it also led, eventually, to a complete change in the constitution of the district. The site of the station was on the boundary between the parishes of Heathfield and Waldron which, during the previous thousand years, had come under different divisions, different rapes, different Poor Law unions, different sanitary authorities and different rural district councils.[1] As the commercial centre developed around the station, with Heathfield High Street actually in the parish of Waldron, it is probably sensible that the whole district is now administered by one council.

The station was partly in a cutting and the approach road bridged the railway just before the line entered a 265 yards long tunnel at the northern end. Although the line reverted to single track between the roadbridge and the tunnel mouth, the headshunt continued through the tunnel to a buffer stop just outside the other end. Most of this long headshunt was lifted soon after the end of the Second World War. The station building was of similar size to those

A similar view about 1920. The fencing in front of the station has been modernised and the diagonal bracing of the footbridge has been boarded over. Plans for the shed occupied by Glynde Creameries Ltd. were submitted in 1919 and included the provision of a footpath to the up platform. The bracket signal at the throat of the goods yard carries four shunting arms. A starting signal is at the end of the down platform but, being directly in line with the yard signals in this view, it is not immediately obvious. *Lens of Sutton*

at Hellingly and Waldron but to a reversed design with the entrance porch and offices to the right of the station master's residence. It was at road level and to one side of the bridge with access to the platforms by a covered footbridge linked to the rear of the building by a gallery.

Originally the footbridge was open at the sides but in 1891 it was agreed by the Engineering Committee that glass should be fitted at a cost of £40.[2] It is interesting to note that a similar proposal for Ardingly, four years earlier, was refused on the grounds that 'the work would create an inconvenient precedent'[3] and shortly after that the same work was agreed at West Hoathly subject to a £20 contribution from the residents of the area. Most of the footbridge at Heathfield was removed in 1939, leaving only the gallery and the stairway to the down platform. From that date access to the up platform was by the roadbridge and a footpath cut into the embankment on the up side.

Waiting rooms and other offices were provided in timber buildings on both platforms. The station building lost its Tudor appearance during 1890 when a Mr. J. Luxford was authorised to carry out repairs and renovation including weather-tiling of the external walls at a cost of £215 14s 0d.[4] Another £435 was spent later in the year when Joseph Longley built a pair of cottages above the tunnel, for the use of railway staff.[5] About the same time a Mr. Giles, coal and coke merchant of Heathfield, had, in erecting a building at Heathfield, encroached upon the company's land by about four or five square yards under the impression that his boundary went to the quickset hedge instead of to the fence only.[6] It was agreed to allow

the building to stand, subject to the payment of one shilling per year, if demanded, to protect the company's rights.

It was not uncommon, in the latter part of the nineteenth century, for a station master to act also as the local

Heathfield station building in August 1969, four years after closure to passenger traffic. At some time in the later years it has been necessary to rebuild one of the chimney stacks and there has obviously been no regard for the aesthetic effect. Perhaps the appearance of the building had already been spoiled by the ugly addition of the bookstall. The pattern of hung tiles at this station, alternately four rows of plain tiles and three rows of decorative tiles, continued up to the peak of the end gable, but there were plain tiles only in the front and rear gables. *Author*

'D1' class 0—4—2 tank No. 296 drawing into Heathfield with a Tunbridge Wells to Eastbourne train. The rear of the station booking hall and other offices, obscured by the gallery to the footbridge, was identical in style to the platform elevation of the other four stations. The gallery appears almost to be an afterthought and although the original drawings show it in plan there is no indication of it on any of the elevations. *Lens of Sutton*

Evidence of the poultry traffic from Heathfield. By the time of this photograph, thought to be in the late thirties, the poultry was sent by ordinary passenger train. The nameboard is an interesting example of the LBSC style with the raised seriffed letters. *Collection Paul Ellis*

Heathfield box viewed from the south. By this date, 1965, a single slip only connects the back siding.   *John Scrace*

postmaster and in 1893 this occurred at Heathfield. Communication between the house and the booking office was provided and a counter supplied so that the station master could take up the appointment of sub-postmaster.[7]

Two further pairs of cottages for railway staff were built in 1897, next to the station building, in the approach road.[8] Until the end of 1902 this road was the property of the railway company and maintenance of it was put out to private contract. The contractor's failure to carry out his obligations led to complaints about the condition of the road in 1897. The local authority had declined to undertake maintenance and the dispute continued for some five years before the company brought the road up to standard and the Uckfield District Council were able to declare it a public road.[9]

As at Hailsham and Waldron, two signal boxes were provided. The larger box, which was on the down side at the Southern end of the station, was known as Heathfield South until the north box was reduced to the status of a ground frame. Originally it was equipped with a frame of twenty-two levers but two additional levers, numbered A and 23, were fitted on 23rd April 1914 to control extra ground signals. These were provided following a minor derailment earlier that year. By 1947 the signalling had been simplified and the distant signals were fixed allowing five levers, numbered 1, 16, 17, 18 and 22, to become spare. After the line closed to passenger traffic on 14th June 1965, the box was reduced to ground frame status and catered for the goods trains which continued to use the line

as far as Heathfield for a further three years. The very last train ran on 26th April 1968 and the box closed on 6th May.

The small box, formerly known as Heathfield North, was at the northern end of the down platform and was equipped with a frame of ten levers. At some date unknown it was reduced to ground frame status and eventually closed on 14th June 1965.

By comparison with the other stations on the line, the goods yard was quite extensive and extra sidings were added during 1896.[10] There were facilities for coal, cattle and general merchandise, a bay platform for horse-boxes and an end loading dock for road vehicles. In its original form the goods warehouse had decorative timbered panels in the walls to match the earlier style of the station building and much of this survived to the end of its existence. The growing importance of Heathfield as a commercial centre is illustrated, perhaps, by the need, in 1921, to enlarge the goods office by some fifty per cent.[11] The warehouse was equipped with a 30 cwt crane and another was provided in the yard. The yard crane had a direct lifting capacity of 4 tons 11 cwt but with the use of a snatch block this could be increased to 7 tons.[12] This additional lifting capacity was probably essential in coping with the needs of the Baltic Saw Mills who conducted their business in the area. The mills' own tugs transported the timber between the railway yard and their own premises. Another regular item of incoming traffic consisted of consignments of bricks for Messrs. Allcorn, a firm of builders, whose own men

On 1st June 1957 a South-Eastern 'C' class 0–6–0 No. 31272 was responsible for the down goods from Tunbridge Wells. It is seen *above* in the yard at Heathfield and *below* departing from Heathfield with just two wagons and a brake van.

Peter Hay

BR Standard class 2—6—4T No. 80089 approaching Heathfield with the 12.45 from Eastbourne to Heathfield on 11th June 1965.

John Scrace

unloaded the railway wagons and transported the bricks to their own yard on the other side of Station Road. In the days of privately owned wagons, those of Hall & Co. of Croydon, and Ward & Son of Tunbridge Wells, carried much of the domestic coal, and the wagons of Stephenson Clarke would have been common, especially during LBSCR days.

A private siding on the down side was shared by Messrs. Stricklands, who owned the corn mill, and the Heathfield and District Poulterers Association. This siding was not to be used for the traffic of any other firm or individual and it was protected by a scotch block[13] at the clearance point with the main line. On average Stricklands received and despatched two wagons each day during the late Brighton and early Southern Railway period[14] and reference has already been made to the special arrangements for the poultry traffic. According to local recollections, live chickens were brought in by rail from all over the place to

The large signal box at Heathfield differed from the one at Hailsham in several respects. It was slightly larger, being 1 ft greater in both width and length, and the floor was 6 inches higher. There was less timber framing below the windows but this was probably due to repair work having been carried out at some time. *Collection John Minnis*

This aerial view of Heathfield seems to tell the same story as the others of the 1959 period. There is little in the goods yard and coal appears to be the only revenue earner.

R. G. Spalding

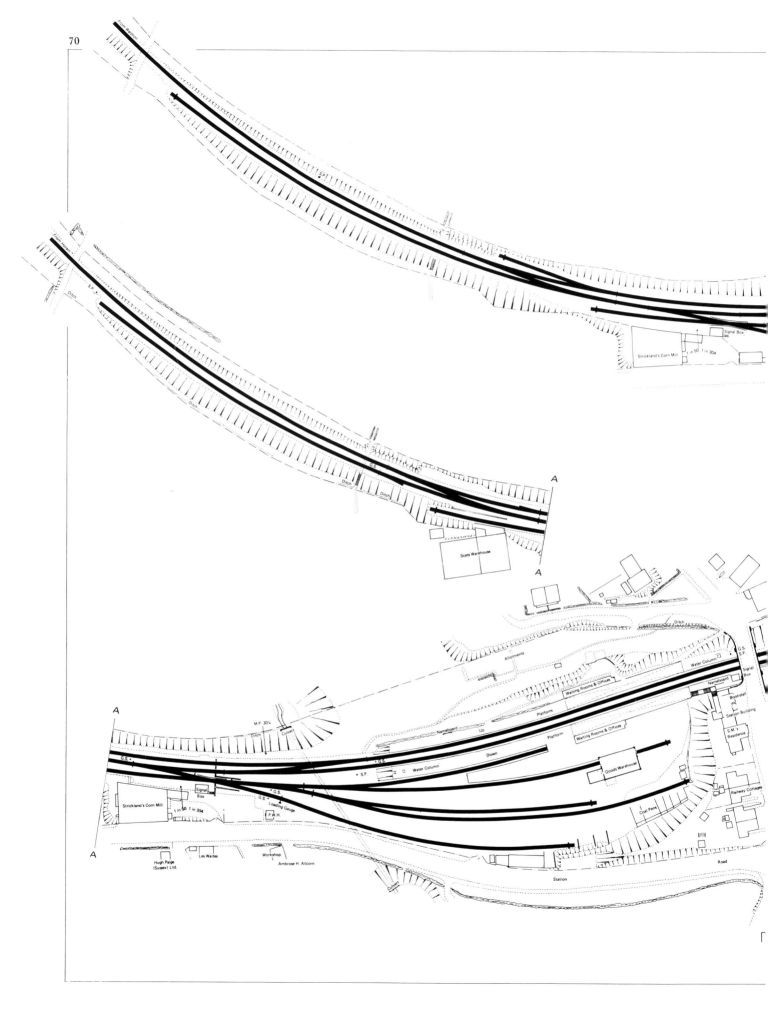

HEATHFIELD 1910

HEATHFIELD c.1961

100   0   100   200   300
SCALE FEET

BR Standard class 2–6–4T No. 80089 again at Heathfield with the 1.40 p.m. to Eastbourne on 11th June 1965. *John Scrace*

be fattened on a mixture of sour milk, ground oats and rendered down fat. It is not certain how long the poultry vans lasted but chicken fattening continued until about 1960. It was an industry that expanded with the coming of the railway but its beginnings were long before the railway age.

Locomotives were able to replenish with water at Heathfield from water columns at the end of each platform. These were supplied from a storage tank which was situated between the roadbridge and the tunnel mouth. Water was drawn from a 370 ft deep bore hole but, because of the high geographical position of Heathfield, the water level fluctuated considerably and it was liable to run dry during any long dry period. In 1896 it was decided to deepen the bore hole in order to alleviate the problem and this was when a reservoir of natural gas was discovered. The gas appears to have been considered a nuisance rather than an asset to begin with but in April 1899 authority was given for 'the utilisation of natural gas for the lighting of Heathfield station' at an estimated cost of £60 for mains and burners etc.[15] No immediate attempt was made to further exploit the find, however, until in May 1902 a company calling itself 'Natural Gas Fields of England Limited' was incorporated with a nominal capital of £100,000 in £1 shares.[16] By September of that year £4,500 had been paid up on the 5,000 shares which had been issued and £1,113 5s. 3d had been spent on boring operations. Pumping apparatus was installed in the tower which supported the water storage tank. In the same month the solicitors for the railway company submitted an engrossment of an agreement to be

Mr. Arthur Powell, formerly station master at Horam, remained in charge at Heathfield until his retirement in the early 1950s.
Collection Paul Ellis

Although the creamery is still in evidence in this view, the name is no longer on the roof. There was some dispute between the railway company and Glynde Creameries in 1921 over a lack of compliance with the agreement. *Collection John Scrace*

entered into with the gas company whereunder a piece of land adjoining Heathfield station was to be let to the gas company for the erection of a gas holder. This was to be at a quarterly rent of £2 10s 0d until 25th December 1903 and thereafter at £5 a quarter, and with the authority to lay two pipes under the railway from this land at an acknowledgement rent of ten shillings per annum.[17] A

published illustration of 1903 shows the gas holder, prominently labelled 'NATURAL GAS' but there is no trace of it on the 1910 edition of the Ordnance Survey map and in 1919 the site appears to have been put to another use.[18] Some doubt has been expressed as to whether this gas holder ever existed and it has been suggested that the photograph was faked for advertisement purposes.

The small signal box at the northern end of the station contained 10 levers. By the time of this photograph, in 1965, the starter signal was carried on a Southern Railway rail-built post. The arm of the water crane has been cranked upwards to allow easier filling of the high tanks of the British Railways standard classes of locomotives. *John Scrace*

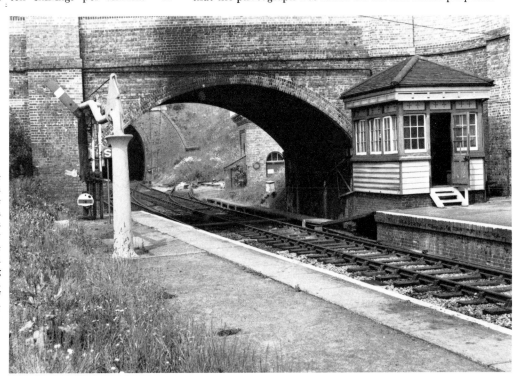

The water tank and the tower which housed the gas pumping apparatus, together with the two small gas holders. *Lens of Sutton*

The gas company certainly had ambitious plans for distributing the gas, however, for in October 1902 they applied to the railway company for permission to lay a twelve inch pipe along the railway line from Heathfield to Polegate to enable them to supply natural gas in that district. They would pay to the railway company an annual wayleave rent of £25 for each mile of pipe and supply gas to the railway company, free of charge, at all the existing or future stations in the district. In addition, the railway company would be compensated for any loss of revenue from coal traffic.[19]

The railway company wished to have the right to terminate the agreement upon the expiration of fifty years,[20] should they so determine, but the gas company

Left: The gas bore. *Above:* The burner. *Collection Paul Ellis*

objected to the railway company alone having this right and it was agreed that either party should have powers of determination on 25th December 1952 or at any subsequent quarter-day upon six months notice being given.[21] The plans of Natural Gas Fields of England Limited were, apparently, over-ambitious for in spite of another organisation, The Natural Gas and Power Company, taking a majority shareholding during the year, they were unable to meet their liabilities. A statement of intention to wind up the company was issued on 3rd December 1903 and it finally ceased to exist on 19th December 1907.

In August 1908 the solicitors again submitted an engrossment of an agreement with the East Sussex Gas Light Coke and Water Company prepared at the request of the general manager, whereunder the gas company would be permitted, for a term of twenty-one years, subject to determination in certain events, to take and use the natural gas rising from the company's well at Heathfield and supply the company with such natural gas or coal gas as may reasonably be required for lighting that station and premises, the gas company paying a royalty for the natural gas at the rate of one shilling and sixpence per thousand cubic feet, with provision for increase or decrease in proportion to the gas company's charge for coal gas to their general customers, and with other provisions to protect the company's interests. The agreement was approved and sealed on 5th August 1908,[22] and then a couple of months later there arose again the prospect of a pipe along the side of the railway. This time it was proposed to lay a six inch pipe between Rotherfield and Polegate and it was agreed that the gas company should be allowed to do so under the same terms and conditions as those embodied in the agreement of 1903 with Natural Gas Fields of England Limited.[23] The matter was referred to the solicitors to complete but in December it was reported that the gas company had declined the terms and the matter, therefore, was at an end.[24] The East Sussex Gas, Light, Coke and Water Company became insolvent in 1913 and the agreement relating to the supply and use of natural gas, sanctioned in August, 1908, was terminated.[25] The gas was of a very high quality, however, being 95% pure methane, and it was of great value for research into mine safety. A gas bottling plant was set up by the water tower and, although Heathfield station continued to make use of the natural gas, most of it went for research purposes, the bottles being transported in open wagons. In 1934 the station was converted to use town gas and from that date until 1963, when the supply dwindled, all of the natural gas was bottled and taken to be used in research.

The site of the gas holder previously referred to was later occupied by a dairy. In 1919 an existing concrete patch was extended and a shed erected by the railway company for the tenancy of Glynde Creameries Limited.[26] During the following two years further sheds were erected and the site was improved, but during 1921 there was a dispute between the two parties with the railway company claiming that the dairy had not complied with the agreement. It is not clear how the matter was resolved but the name of the dairy does not feature on the shed roof in the later photographs.

Heathfield station was the winner of two competitions in the post-war years. In 1955 it was judged to be the best kept station but how rapidly neglect takes its toll. After the closure of the line in 1965 the station site became Heathfield's black spot and won the first prize in a competition to find the worst station site in Sussex. In 1979 Wealden District Council became the owner of the site and there are plans to develop it as an estate for light industry.

Another view of No. 80089 at Heathfield on 11th June 1965.
John Scrace

1   An item in the *Sussex Express* on 31st January 1880 under the heading 'WALDRON — OUR STATION' refers to our new station situate in the Parish of Waldron and goes on to describe the new Heathfield station.
2   Engineering Committee Meeting: 15.12.1891. Minute 6.
3   ,,   ,,   ,,   22.6.1887. Minute 4.
4   ,,   ,,   ,,   20.5.1890. Minute 3.
5   ,,   ,,   ,,   7.10.1890. Minute 11.
6   ,,   ,,   ,,   4.11.1890. Minute 7.
7   ,,   ,,   ,,   16.5.1893. Minute 7.
8   ,,   ,,   ,,   13.10.1897. Min. 10.
9   ,,   ,,   ,,   21.9.1899. Minute 17.
       ,,   ,,   ,,   18.12.1901. Min. 10.
       ,,   ,,   ,,   9.4.1902. Minute 9.
       ,,   ,,   ,,   8.10.1902. Minute 1.
10 Half-Yearly Report: June 1896.
11 Engineering Committee Meeting: 21.4.1920. Minute 11.
12 1934 Appendix to the Working Timetable.
13   ,,   ,,   ,, ,,   ,,   ,,
14 1921   ,,   ,, ,,   ,,   ,,
15 Engineering Committee Meeting: 26.4.1899. Minute 8.
16 Registration Certification No. 73815.
17 Engineering Committee Meeting: 24.9.1902. Minute 9.
18 Gray, James S. Victorian & Edwardian Sussex, Plate 92.
19 Engineering Committee Meeting: 8.10.1902. Minute 13.
20   ,,   ,,   ,,   21.1.1903. Minute 11.
21   ,,   ,,   ,,   28.1.1903. Minute 12.
22   ,,   ,,   ,,   5.8.1908. Minute 6.
23   ,,   ,,   ,,   14.10.1908. Minute 8.
24   ,,   ,,   ,,   9.12.1908. Minute 22.
25   ,,   ,,   ,,   12.2.1913. Minute 8.
26   ,,   ,,   ,,   21.5.1919. Minute 5.

No. 2002 with the 4.39 p.m. train from Eastbourne to Tunbridge Wells leaving Heathfield tunnel on 12th May 1951.

S. C. Nash

'C2X' No. 32543, approaching Heathfield tunnel with the down goods on 30th July 1951.

S. C. Nash

'J' class 4—6—2 tank No. 32325, formerly named *Abergavenny*, makes an effortless climb to Heathfield tunnel with the 11.08 a.m. Victoria to Eastbourne train on 2nd September 1949. Nos. 32325 and 32326 were permitted to work the Heathfield line from April 1944 but neither were regular users of the line until the summer timetable of 1949 introduced the through train from Victoria.

S. C. Nash

The approach to Mayfield from Heathfield in 1928.

O. J. Morris, cty. E. Jackson

Mayfield station in LBSCR days including the small signal box on the up platform. Rotherfield, from a similar viewpoint, would have appeared almost identical.   *Lens of Sutton*

MAYFIELD

Although the station at Mayfield was quite conveniently situated, the railway appears to have had little effect upon the village it served. Whereas the village of Heathfield was some distance from the railway but became absorbed by the town which developed around the station, no such growth seems to have occurred at Mayfield. The main street, which is noted for its charm and interest, drops down the hill from the village and continues as Station Road until the station approach is reached. Reference to the various editions of the 25 inch series of Ordnance Survey maps will show little development in the vicinity of the station and the only real differences between the pre-railway First Edition of 1874 and the Second Edition of 1899, apart from the railway itself, are the Station Hotel and the gas works. The gas works were at a higher level than the railway and there was no possibiity of a rail link for direct deliveries of coal or the despatch of by-products from gas manufacture, which were presumably roaded the few hundred yards between the goods yard and the gas works.

The station building was on the down platform and was similar in style to those already discussed but, in common with that at Rotherfield, the building was of greater length in order to accommodate refreshment rooms, a kitchen and a porter's and lamp room. A cellar was provided under the refreshment room with access by trap doors both within the serving area and outside the building. Why refreshment facilities were considered necessary at Mayfield and Rotherfield and not at the three other new stations is not clear.[1]

Some alteration to the building was authorised when the station master's house was in need of renovation in 1889. The yard was covered over to provide a scullery and the copper and sink were removed from the kitchen, allowing this room to be used also as a dining room. At the same time the exposed end of the house was weather-tiled to cover the original Tudor style and the estimated cost of this work was £44.[2] Two years later a further £146 was authorised to be spent on renovation and this probably allowed for the remaining part of the station master's house to be tile-hung.[3] Apart from these alterations, the building remained much the same for the rest of its railway existence and the entrance porch was the only one of the five along this line to survive in very nearly original condition. The leaded lights with stained glass were still in evidence fifteen years after closure, as were the stained glass toplights to the main windows.

Access to the up platform was by a subway, the stairway for which was just beyond the entrance to the gentlemen's toilet. The stair well was protected from the weather by the platform canopy which was extended beyond the usual length and supported by a screen wall. Behind this screen wall an additional store was built and, although this is indicated on the 1899 edition of the Ordnance Survey map, it is not shown on the original drawings. An early photograph of rather poor quality suggests that the area at that time was partially roofed over and used, perhaps, as a builder's yard. On the up platform there was a small timber waiting shed similar to the one at Waldron. The canopy, however, was extended to shelter the subway stair well and this was supported by a timber screen wall. It will be

Mayfield station in 1929. The small signal box is still sited on the up platform for it was not closed for another two years. The large box would have been just off the picture to the right.

Aerofilms Ltd.

It will be noticed that the decorative fretwork has gone from the waiting room end wall in this c.1960 view. The new brick-built box enclosing the lever frame can be seen under the canopy on the down platform.   *Collection John Minnis*

evident from some of the illustrations that the roof was considerably altered from the original and this was done at some time between 1929 and 1950. As at Waldron, the shed was partly open to the platform but it was probably closed in and given a door during the early 1890s when similar work was carried out at other stations.

Although in the same style as those at the other stations, the two signal boxes at Mayfield differed from them, each in a distinctive way. Mayfield North, the larger box with a 22-lever frame, was set back into the embankment, and in order to afford the signalman a good view of the line, it was taller than usual with a floor height of twelve feet, eight inches. The stairway descended towards the track as at Hailsham but, because of the extra floor height, there was no problem of obstruction to the door to the lower floor. The small signal box, Mayfield South, contained a 12-lever frame. It was sited on the up platform and was different in that the base was of timber construction, although this would not have been very obvious because most of it was below platform level. According to one source, both of the signal boxes date from the opening of the line, but the south box is not shown on a railway survey of 1889 and, as it is shown on the 1899 edition of the Ordnance Survey map, it seems likely that it was provided during that decade. Both boxes were closed on 24th September 1931, and a 22-lever frame was provided on the down platform, in front of the booking office, and surrounded by an iron railing. The block instruments were also moved to the booking office and the duties of signalman and porter were combined. A closing switch was

provided and when the box was closed all trains used the down platform. A miniature staff was used at these times for the section between Rotherfield and Heathfield. During the British Railways period the iron railing was replaced by a brick and timber cabin similar to the one at Horam. For this cabin direct access from the booking office was provided.

An earlier view of the lever frame on the down platform which was similar to the one at Waldron. The iron railings were replaced in the late 1950s by the brick-built structure featured above, and a door was cut through to the booking office. *Author's collection*

Up Platform

Waiting Shed

Subway

Signal Box

Down Platform

Nameboard

Carriage Dock

S.P.

Nameboard

Station Building

S.M.'s Residence

Goods Warehouse

Goods Yard

Coal

Pens

Lane

Love

Road

Road

S.P.

1 in 50 LEVEL

Ditch

Ditch

Lewes

Ditch

Ditch

M.P. 34

From Heathfield

Culvert

Ditch

Ditch

The Railway Hotel

Gas Works

Steps

Up Platform

Milk Stand

Waiting Shed

Subway

Down Platform

Nameboard

Goods Yard

Nameboard

Signal Box

Garage

Goods Warehouse

S.M.'s Residence

Station Building

Coal

Allotments

South Eastern Farmers

Ditch

Road

Road

Station

Road

Lewes

S.P.

1 in 50 LEVEL

Ditch

Ditch

South Eastern Gas Board

M.P. 34

Shed

Shed

Shed

Shed

Sub Station

From Heathfield

Sand Drag

Culvert

Ditch

Ditch

The Railway Hotel

Ditch

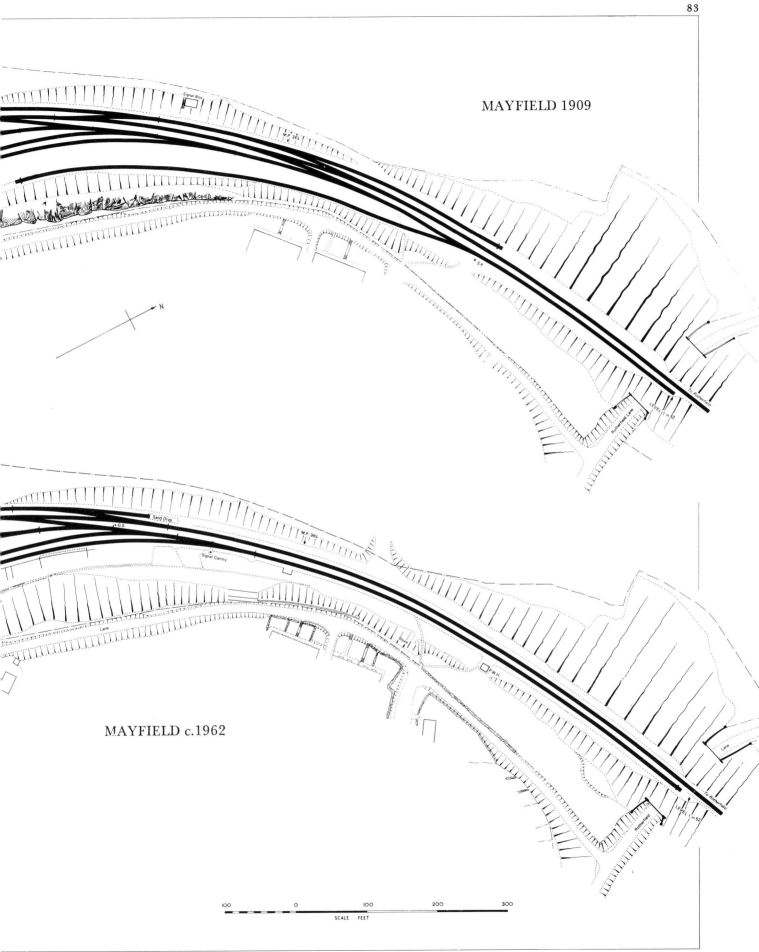

MAYFIELD 1909

N

MAYFIELD c.1962

100   0   100   200   300

SCALE   FEET

The northern end of the station about 1960 showing the screens at the northern end of the canopies. *Collection John Minnis*

Except for the absence of the moulded panels above the windows, this was the appearance of the entrance porch to all the five new stations when they were built and for most of their existence. Neither Hellingly nor Waldron had the attractive ridge tiles, however. The original drawings indicate that the porches at Hellingly and Heathfield extended further from the building with a fourth window but it is certain that they were all built as shown in this study at Mayfield. Here the pattern of hung tiles, from the bottom upwards, was six rows of plain tiles followed by bands of four rows of decorative tiles and five rows of plain tiles alternately. This pattern continued up to the peak of the front and rear gables but there were plain tiles only on the end gable. *Author*

Mayfield. Argos Hill.

The north box at Mayfield was tucked into the embankment and this necessitated a floor height of 12 ft 8 ins, at least four feet higher than any of the other boxes.
Lens of Sutton

Siding accommodation was quite generous in the earlier years but by 1931 one of the sidings had been lifted, leaving facilities similar to those at Rotherfield. There were sidings for coal and general goods and, although there was no crane in the yard, there was one of 30 cwt in the goods warehouse. This warehouse was of similar size and design to those at Heathfield and Rotherfield but the decorative patterns in the panels were different with floral designs instead of diagonal timbers. Numerous coats of paint tended to obscure the fact that much of this decoration survived right through to modern times. The goods yard was closed on 17th June 1963.

At its peak the milk traffic, which was probably the most important source of revenue at Mayfield, amounted to some 300,000 gallons a year and there were special arrangements for its transport. In 1932 the engine of the up goods left its train at Rotherfield and returned light to Mayfield in order to attach milk vans to the 9.50 a.m. passenger train from Eastbourne. This practice continued until 1937 but with a variation from 1933 to 1935 in that the engine continued down the line to Heathfield, after attaching the milk vans to the passenger train, before returning to Rotherfield to continue with its goods train to Tunbridge Wells. It has not been possible to find the reason for this curious practice and by 1938 it was discontinued altogether, allowing the daily goods to arrive at Tunbridge Wells one hour earlier. By 1950, as at Horam, the milk traffic had been lost to road transport.

The goods warehouse at Mayfield differed from the ones at Rotherfield and Heathfield by having a more symmetrical design to the end wall.
Author

1 The *Sussex Express*: 15.10.1881. It was reported in this edition of the newspaper that The County Licensing Committee at Lewes had confirmed the grant of a licence for the refreshment rooms at Heathfield although no other reference has been found to such a facility at that station.
2 Engineering Committee Meeting: 21.5.1889. Minute 5.
3   ,,   ,,   ,, 30.6.1891. Minute 1.

A Mogul was a very rare sight on the Cuckoo Line in the 'thirties but in June 1933 'N' class 2–6–0 No. 1868 heads a sight-seeing excursion train near Mayfield. Included in the formation is a clerestory-roofed Pullman car.

Dr. Ian C. Allen

'C2X' class 0—6—0 No. 32538 near Mayfield on 20th August 1951, in charge of the Polegate to Tunbridge Wells goods train.   *S. C. Nash*

'H' class 0—4—4T No. 31518 with the 10.45 a.m. Eastbourne to Tunbridge Wells train climbing from Mayfield on 3rd June 1962. *S. C. Nash*

On 12th June 1950 'J2' class 4—6—2T No. 32326 is seen at the head of the 11.08 Victoria to Eastbourne train at Argos Hill near Rotherfield.

S. C. Nash

'C2X' class 0—6—0 No. 32534 at Argos Hill with the down goods from Tunbridge Wells on 19th September 1950.

S. C. Nash

No. 80010 at Argos Hill on 2nd June 1962, with the 10.39 a.m.
Tunbridge Wells to Eastbourne train.   *S. C. Nash*

'E5' class 0—6—2T No. 32585 at Argos Hill, near Rotherfield, working the 1.50 p.m. Tunbridge Wells to Eastbourne train on 9th April 1952. This locomotive was withdrawn in May 1954.

A view of the station looking from the up platform towards the south. The roof seen through the canopy of the up platform belongs to the shop shown in the illustration on page 95.

Lens of Sutton

ROTHERFIELD & MARK CROSS

Until the line from Tunbridge Wells to Eastbourne was opened throughout on 1st August 1880, Rotherfield was the name given to the present Crowborough and Jarvis Brook station. The village of Rotherfield was about three-quarters of a mile to the south-west of the new railway and double that distance from the station that previously bore its name. Mark Cross is a small village about a mile and a half to the north-east of the station at a point where the B2100 road from Rotherfield crosses the A267 road to Eastbourne. The site chosen for the new station was at a place known as Town Row where there were a few cottages at a road junction.

The station was built on a left-hand curve, in the northerly direction, of thirty-two chains radius and the layout was very similar to that at Mayfield. The station building on the down platform was almost identical and the only obvious difference from Mayfield was the absence of a screen wall to support an extended canopy. At Rotherfield the stair well for the subway to the up platform was in front of the booking office. No direct reference to the weather-tiling of the station master's residence has been found but in 1891 a Mr. Harman was authorised to carry out renovation work at an estimated cost of £165.[1] The other stations were altered about this time and the quoted price would seem to be sufficient to cover the cost. The waiting shed on the up platform was similar to those at

Waldron and at Mayfield but the canopy was extended to the left of the shed in order to shelter the different position of the subway stair well. Both platforms were equipped with a water column but it has not been possible to establish whether there was a water storage tank and it is interesting that in 1892 a Mr. George Wray agreed to supply water to the station for a further five years at an increased charge of £25 per annum.[2]

The larger box, Rotherfield North, was on the up side, opposite the goods yard, and it contained a frame of twenty-two levers. The floor height was 8 ft 4 ins and the stairway descended parallel to the track. At the other end of the station the small box, Rotherfield South, was sited on the ramp of the down platform. In line with the economy measures of the 1930s, the north box was closed on 22nd December 1935, and the block instruments were moved to the south box, which was then renamed Rotherfield. Probably at the same time the twelve-lever frame was extended or replaced to provide nineteen levers. This box survived to the closure of the line, probably because the position of the subway stair well precluded the siting of a lever frame on the platform as at Mayfield and Waldron.

At the southern end of the station, the line crossed the B2100 road on a stone-built bridge. Several buildings had stood in the path of the railway and one of these survived the construction of the line to abut against the retaining

Although the nameboard is original, the enamelled sign 'ROTHERFIELD' is unusual for the period, as is the omission of the 'MARK CROSS' part of the name. Note the early provision of the screen at the southern end of the up platform canopy. No such protection has been provided on the down side as at Mayfield.

Collection John Minnis

Rotherfield and Mark Cross station during LBSCR days. The building was virtually the same as that at Mayfield but with a different pattern of hung tiles. At this station the bands consisted of six rows of plain tiles, then six rows of decorative tiles followed by four rows of each alternately up to the peak of the gable. The end wall over the booking hall had plain tiles only. The gables over the entrance porch and the ladies room retain the Tudor appearance at this time. *Lens of Sutton*

The platform side of the station at about the same period as the previous illustration. *Lens of Sutton*

An aerial view c.1959.

Rotherfield Station

The remote siting of the station at Rotherfield is well illustrated in this view. One of the pairs of railway cottages may be seen on the slope behind the station building.
Collection John Minnis

wall of the bridge. It was railway property and in use as a shop. A new shop front was authorised in 1907 at an estimated cost of £50 19s 6d.

The goods facilities were much the same as those to be seen at Mayfield although the latter station had an extra siding in the early days. The earlier track plans show some complicated pointwork in the connections with the goods yard and these connections seem to have been modified on several occasions. The provision of additional access to the carriage dock was discussed at the Engineering Committee Meeting on 6th October 1891.[3] The work was authorised and it was completed by 3rd May, 1892.[4] Other plans of 1899 indicate a further complication of the pointwork. The goods warehouse, of the same size and style as that at Heathfield, was equipped with a 30 cwt crane but, like Mayfield, there was no crane in the yard. There is a curious reference in the Engineering Committee Minute Book, dated 17th January 1888, to the rebuilding of the warehouse out of old materials at a cost of £41 but it is thought that some other building must have been under discussion.[5]

Reference has already been made to the lack of industry in the area whilst nothing has been found relating to any specific items, but the goods traffic must have been quite brisk for, in the early part of this century, it was necessary for a daily goods train to work up the line as far as Rotherfield in addition to the through goods. One of the illustrations shows twenty wagons in the part of the yard that is visible. By the middle of the 1930s the second goods train had been discontinued but this may not necessarily have been the result of a reduction in the volume of traffic. Extensive work in Oxted Tunnel was the reason for some interesting operations at Rotherfield in 1921 and 1922. The through goods terminated at Rotherfield during this time and the engine of a goods train from Tunbridge Wells to Brighton was diverted to Rotherfield to collect wagons for

Eridge and beyond. The timetable reverted to normal in October 1922.

The station was closed on 14th June 1965, and Crowborough became the nearest railway station for the village of Rotherfield once again.

1. Engineering Committee Meeting: 21.4.1891. Minute 3.
2. ,, ,, ,, 8.3.1892. Minute 5.
3. ,, ,, ,, 6.10.1891. Minute 3.
4. ,, ,, ,, 3.5.1892. Minute 2.
   Half-Yearly Report, June 1892.
5. Engineering Committee Meeting: 17.1.1888. Minute 3.

The shop built into the retaining wall of the bridge was the surviving building at the end of a terrace which occupied this site before the arrival of the railway in 1880.
Author

A

A

Trough
Well
Culvert
Sluice
Footbridge
Culvert
Pipe
Ditch
M.P. 36¾
Shop &
Post
Office
Drain
S.P.
Water Column
Signal Box
1 in 50 LEVEL
Nameboard
Subway
Up Platform
Waiting Shed
Retaining Wall
Retaining Wall
Ditch
Pipe
Ditch
Water Column
S
Station Building
S.M's
Residence
Down Platform
Nameboard
Carriage Dock
Goods Yard
Goods Warehouse
Coal Yard

From Mayfield
Culvert
S.P.
A
Ditch
To Mayfield
Railway Inn
A
Cottages
Station Building

To Milk Cross

To Rotherfield
Hill
Footbridge
Sub Station
Ditch
Packham
Cottages
T.C.B.
Footbridge
Trough
Well
Culvert
Sluice
Culvert
Pipe
Ditch
Ditch
Pipe
Retaining Wall
Retaining Wall
Ditch
Pipe
From Mayfield
M.P. 36¾
Sand Drag
Shop &
Post
Office
Drain
Nameboard
S.P.
Waiting Shed
Up Platform
Signal Box
Water Column
1 in 50 LEVEL
Lamp Room
Subway
Water Column
S.P.
Station Building
Residence
Down Platform
Nameboard
S.S.
Culvert
Ditch
Ditch
Ditch
Goods Yard
Goods Warehouse
Loading
Coal Yard
G.P.
Cottages
Pipe
Ditch
Cottages

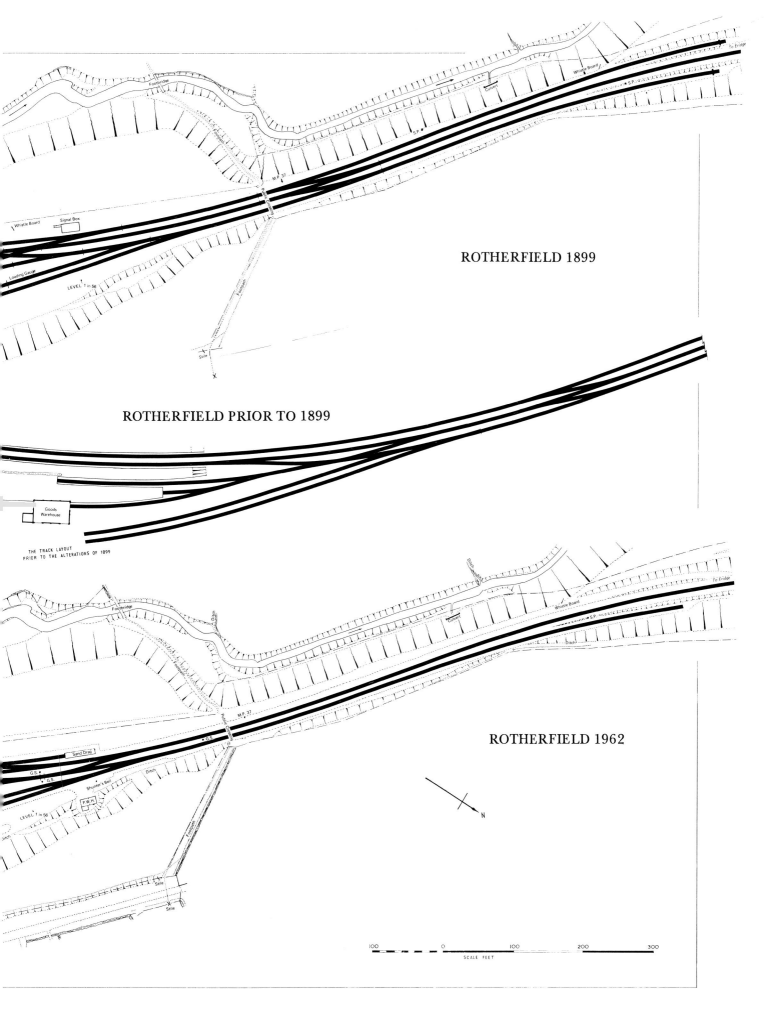

ROTHERFIELD 1899

ROTHERFIELD PRIOR TO 1899

THE TRACK LAYOUT
PRIOR TO THE ALTERATIONS OF 1899

ROTHERFIELD 1962

N

100   0   100   200   300
SCALE FEET

The goods yard and coal yard during the early 1900s. The timber panels are still evident at this time. The number of wagons in the yard could be evidence of the need for two goods trains per day.

Lens of Sutton

Rotherfield and Mark Cross in 1965, about a month before closure. The water columns have not been modified here as at Heathfield, probably as they were seldom used with the larger engines in use during the final years. *John Scrace*

BR Standard 2—6—4T No. 80034 at Rotherfield with the 8.54 a.m. Eridge to Polegate train on 24th May 1965.

John Scrace

No. 32326, formerly named *Bessborough*, entering Rotherfield with the 11.08 a.m. Victoria to Eastbourne train during 1950. The malachite green applied in 1946 was retained after Nationalisation.

S. C. Nash

Class 'D3' 0—4—4 tank No. 2378, near Rotherfield with a train from Tunbridge Wells to Eastbourne, during 1935.

'N1' class 2—6—0 No. 31878 approaching Rotherfield with the 4.10 p.m. Tonbridge to Eastbourne train on 24th June 1961. *S. C. Nash*

By July 1931 ex-SECR 'H' class 0—4—4 tank No. 1182 was allocated to Redhill and may well still have been at that shed when this photograph was taken in 1935. The 'H' class tanks first appeared on these lines in 1929 with the introduction of the through services from the Eastern section. Nos. A305, A309, A320, A324, A512 and A553 worked the trains from Tonbridge to Brighton or Eastbourne. From about 1937 the 8.10 a.m. Oxted to Eastbourne train worked via the Crowhurst Spur, Tonbridge and Tunbridge Wells and was usually headed by an 'H' class. Mr. Nash also photographed this engine on this line, as 31182, some fifteen years later. *Dr. Ian C. Allen*

REDGATE MILL JUNCTION

When first opened, the single line from Eastbourne ran parallel with the single line from Uckfield between Redgate Mill and Eridge, a distance of a little over a mile and a quarter, forming, in effect, double single track. The junction for the two lines was at Eridge and this situation continued until 1894 when it was decided to double the line to Uckfield. A new junction was installed at Redgate Mill which became the beginning of the section for Eastbourne line trains. The requisite signal box was of timber construction and contained a frame of seventeen levers, five of which were spare. In 1955 the junction was remodelled and eight levers were then spare. Eridge station was responsible for supplying coal to the signal box and this was transported in sacks, when necessary, by the down goods from Tunbridge Wells to Eastbourne. The box closed on 14th June 1965, with the end of the line to Eastbourne.

The view south, showing the Eastbourne line branching off to the left. The signal box, which was of all timber construction, was opened in 1894 for the new junction when the line to Uckfield was doubled. *Lens of Sutton*

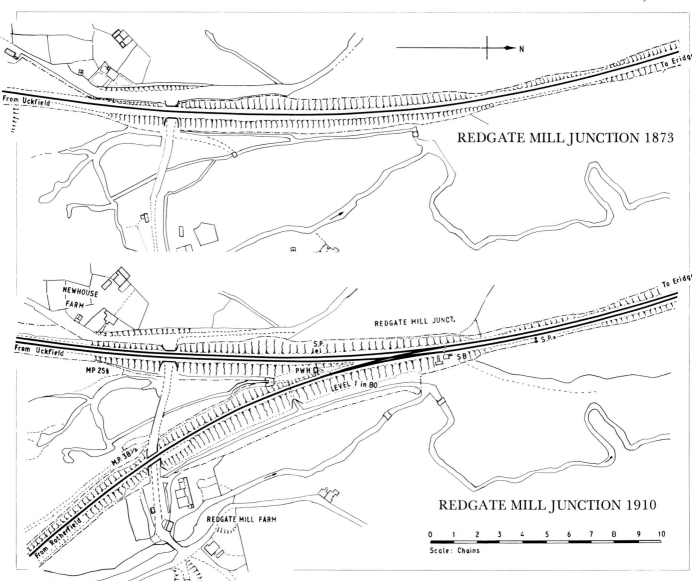

REDGATE MILL JUNCTION 1873

REDGATE MILL JUNCTION 1910

Scale: Chains

The 11.09 a.m. from Victoria to Eastbourne headed by Fairburn 2—6—4T No. 42099, is about to run on to the branch on 31st August 1953.
R. C. Riley

'E4' class 0—6—2 tank No. 32517, taking the Brighton line at Redgate Mill Junction on 31st August 1953. This view shows the junction in its original form (as a double junction) with the Eastbourne lines on the right converging to form single track. This layout was simplified in 1955.
R. C. Riley

'J2' class 4—6—2T No. 32326 and 'I3' class 4—4—2T No. 32089 approaching Eridge with the 9.55 a.m. Eastbourne-Tunbridge Wells West on Easter Monday, 26th March 1951.

R. C. Riley

ERIDGE

Although in recent years the facilities were very much reduced, Eridge continued to serve as the junction for trains working between Uckfield and London or Uckfield and Tonbridge, and, until 12th August 1985, when the section of line between Birchden Junction and Tunbridge Wells was closed, it was still possible to see trains dividing or connecting as they worked the two routes. The station takes its name from Eridge Park, which is over two miles away, and with only two dwellings nearby, The Lodge, which was opposite and pre-dated the railway, and the Railway Hotel, there seems to have been even less reason for its existence than some of the stations already described.

Eridge was opened in 1868 as a very simple station with one platform for the single line. No passing loop was provided and there were no signals or signal box. The goods yard consisted of little more than a headshunt with a siding and a loop which ran through a timber-built goods shed but the layout did allow the yard to be worked by trains in both directions. The station building was at platform level and it is unfortunate that no photographs or drawings have been found to illustrate this period.

With the opening of the line to Eastbourne in 1880, the station was rebuilt with two island platforms, one for each route, and the two tracks continued south as parallel single lines to Redgate Mill where the Eastbourne and Brighton

lines diverged. This section of the Eastbourne line actually began its existence as a siding for the use of the contractors which was sanctioned for use on the 24th December 1878, and, to quote the Inspecting Officer: ' . . . the new siding referred to is virtually a portion of a new line now in course of construction called the Tunbridge Wells, Hailsham and Eastbourne Railway, and it is not yet determined whether this new line is to be continued on to Groombridge and thus make two single lines parallel and close alongside each other or to complete the line between these two stations as a continuation of the double line from Tunbridge Wells to Groombridge. A new signal cabin was to be provided and this contained eleven levers. New arrangements were to be made when the line was converted for passenger use and in fact the line to Groombridge was doubled by 1880. The signal cabin proved to be a temporary affair which was replaced by a larger one a little further to the south.

The new station building was on the bridge which carries the A26 road over the line and, although not to the same style or design as those on the Eastbourne line, it did have many features in common with them. The original plans shows the walls above the level of the top of the windows to have been in a Tudor style. No photographic evidence has been found to confirm that it was ever so built, but the

The signal box at the southern end of the station may just be seen through the bridge in this view of Eridge in the early 1900s.

Lens of Sutton

Eridge station on 18th August 1951.

H. C. Casserley

Eridge station was rebuilt in 1880, the building shown here replacing one at platform level. Although not built in the same style as the other stations of the line, it does share many similar features and may well have been a Myers' design. The brickwork above the windows is obviously of a later date, possibly, from 1893 when repair and renovation of the station offices was authorised at an estimated cost of £394. The drawings of 1880 indicate half-timbering above the windows and in a herring-bone pattern in the gables.
John Scrace

illustrations clearly show a difference in brickwork above the window level. It is not certain when the alteration may have been carried out but it may have been included with repairs and renovation at an estimated cost of £394 authorised in 1893.[1] The original drawings also indicate ladies rooms at one end of the building, but if these ever existed they have long been gone. Adjoining the rear of the building there is a timber-built gallery with wooden stairways leading down to the platforms. On each platform there were two buildings of timber construction and these housed refreshment rooms[2] with cellars below, waiting rooms, ladies' rooms, toilets and offices and they were under long canopies which covered most of the platform length. At some time before 1950, the building on the down platform, which included the gentlemen's toilet, was demolished and the canopy was shortened accordingly. The toilet survived, however, and was enclosed within a new timber structure. Three water columns were provided at Eridge with two of them on the down platform and one on the up platform.[3] These were supplied from a water tank which was on the down side to the south of the road bridge. According to the original drawings the tank was supported on a tower of similar design to the one at Heathfield. Water supply was a problem in 1914 with the opening of the Birchden to Ashurst spur and the existing well was deepened by a further 150 feet.

With the enlarging of the station in 1880 and its changed function, signalling and signal boxes were required and it is unfortunate that an incomplete signalling diagram has had to be included for this period. Two signal boxes were provided, one at each end of the station. The south box, with twenty-six levers, was on a brick base with a floor height of 7 ft 6 ins and the stairway descended towards the track. Being 18 ft 6 ins long and 11 ft 6 ins wide, it was similar in its proportions to the new boxes along the Eastbourne line, but as no drawings or photographs have been found, it is not possible to know if it was in the same

style. The north box was also on a brick base but of rather different proportions. Equipped with a thirty-two lever frame, it is 19 ft 6 ins long by 10 ft wide and the stairway descends towards the track from a 5 ft high floor. With the doubling of the track to Uckfield in 1894 there came the need for some modification of the track layout and signalling, and some of the alterations are indicated on the signalling diagram on page 168. The two single lines south of Eridge became normal up and down lines and the two platforms also became directional. There was little or no change from this time until 1930 when Eridge south box was closed on 21st September. From this date the crossover at the southern end of the station was worked from a ground frame and Eridge north box was re-named Eridge. It is still in use to the present day. Eridge was responsible for supplying coal to the signal box at Birchden Junction as well as the one at Redgate Mill Junction. When required, the through goods to or from the Eastbourne line carried the coal, in sacks, to these boxes. Birchden Junction box closed on 12th August 1985, when Eridge lost its link with Tunbridge Wells and from that date the line between Eridge and Hever formed the block section.

The limited goods yard facilities of 1873 were improved with the provision of an additional siding, a five-ton crane and a carriage dock. There were plans for a goods warehouse similar to those at Heathfield, Mayfield and Rotherfield, but they came to nothing and the timber built shed survived until well after closure of the goods yard. Adjacent to the back siding, Turner's Timber Yard carried on its business and there were instructions that this firm's employees were to be warned before any shunting operation took place. The crane used by the firm's men was to be secured in the normal position before shunting began.[4]

The importance of Eridge as an interchange station for through carriages did not begin to develop until after 1914 when the Birchden to Ashurst spur was doubled and brought into use for direct services between London and

The goods shed features in this view of 'U1' class Mogul No. 31896 at Eridge on 2nd April 1956.

R. C. Riley

Fairburn 2—6—4T No. 42101 at Eridge on 18th August 1951.

H. C. Casserley

The view towards Birchden Junction, seen from the footbridge gallery on 20th August 1976.   *John Scrace*

the coast. Although, prior to this date, over 50 passenger trains were handled each weekday, the station was merely a stopping place. With the increasing introduction of through services to London, however, more and more of the through carriage interchanges were transferred from Groombridge to Eridge until, by the 1930s the role of the two stations had been reversed. This pattern continued until the branch line closures of 1965 and a typical example of these interesting workings could have been seen soon after midday on any summer weekday of 1952. A train from London, with carriages for both Eastbourne and Brighton, arrived at Eridge at 12.14 p.m. to be followed a few minutes later by a train from Tunbridge Wells to Brighton. At about the same time a train from Brighton to Tonbridge arrived from the south to provide a connection to Tunbridge Wells for passengers from the London train. After detaching its rear carriages, the train from London continued on to Eastbourne. The locomotive of the Brighton-bound train attached the remaining carriages from London to its own train before continuing its journey. Reference to the various timetables show that similar activities occurred several times during the course of the day. It was a practice that began towards the end of the 'Brighton' period and continued right through Southern Railway days into the second decade of the British Railways period. To a very limited extent it continued up to the loss of the line to Tunbridge Wells.

[1] Engineering Committee Meeting: 6.6.1893. Minute 2.
[2] *The Sussex Express*: 15.10.1881. The County Licensing Committee at Lewes confirmed the grant of a licence.
[3] Appendix to the Working Timetable – 1934.
[4]   ,,   ,, ,,   ,,   ,,   ,,

The signal box at the northern end of the station, although built in 1880, is of a different style from those on the line to Eastbourne. It has a low floor height of only 5 ft and it is 19 ft 6 in long by 10 ft wide with a frame of 32 levers. The 26-lever south box is thought to have been in a similar style, and dimensions were 18 ft 6 in long by 11 ft 6 in wide and with a floor height of 7 ft 6 in. When this box was closed in 1930 the crossover at the southern end of the station was worked by a ground frame.

John Scrace

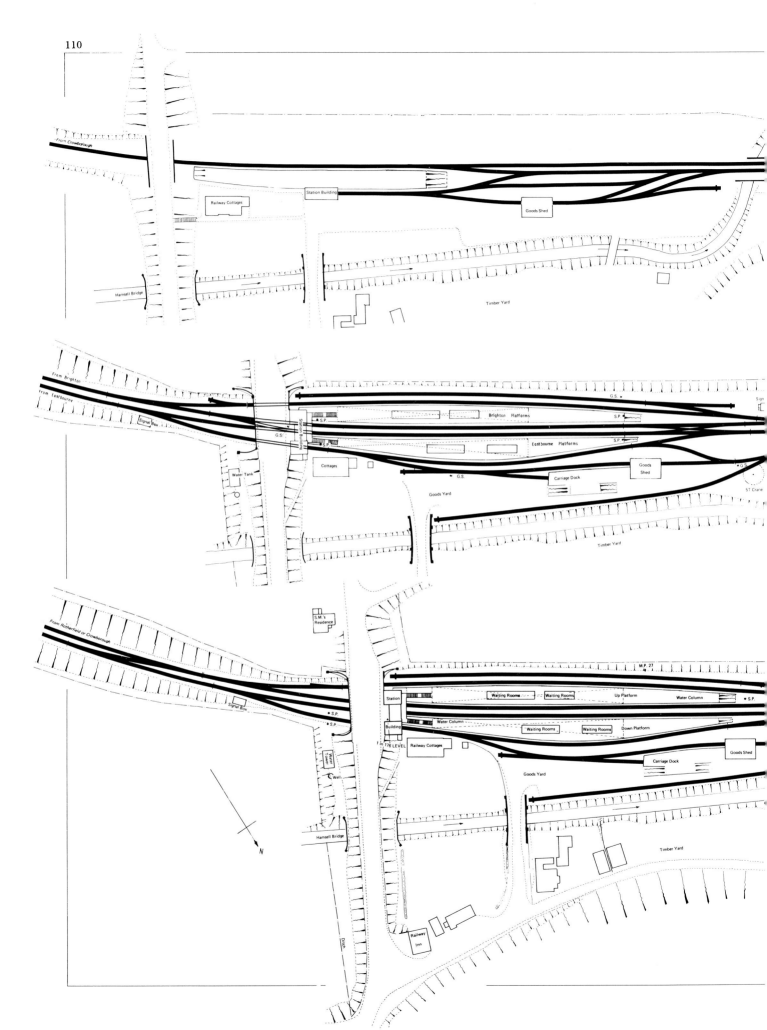

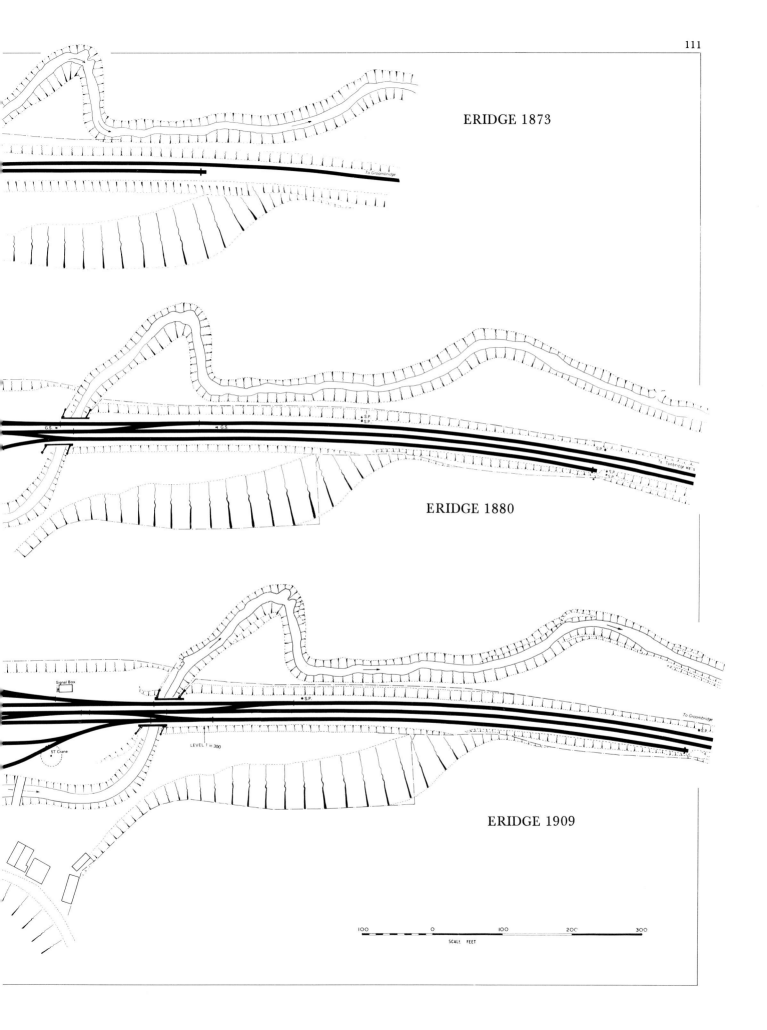

ERIDGE 1873

ERIDGE 1880

ERIDGE 1909

BIRCHDEN JUNCTION

'B2X' class 4—4—0 passes Birchden Junction with a down train in 1929. The number is indecipherable but could be 205 for this locomotive regularly worked a London Bridge to Eastbourne train at this time. Birchden Junction Box closed on 12th August 1985 together with Tunbridge Wells A and B Boxes when the section of line from here to Tunbridge Wells was closed. The line between Eridge and Hever then formed the block section.

Author's Collection

GROOMBRIDGE JUNCTION

'H' class 0—4—4T No. 31164 passing Groombridge Junction Signal Box with a Tunbridge Wells West to Oxted push-pull train on 23rd July 1955. *R. C. Riley*

The signal box at Groombridge Junction, shown here in 1928, was closed in 1958 when the new box was provided at the station. The lines on the left lead to Eridge and those on the right to Oxted and East Grinstead. *O. J. Morris, cty. R. C. Riley*

The 'upside-down' footbridge, second-hand from Battersea.
Author's Collection

Looking towards Groombridge station from the upside-down footbridge in 1928.

O. J. Morris, cty. R. C. Riley

A closer view of the tall junction signals – again in 1928.

O. J. Morris, cty. R. C. Riley

This bridge of unusual design crossed the line at a point where the embankment was higher on one side than the other. Although the gradient was slight, it was apparently felt necessary to provide steps for pedestrians in the middle of the carriageway.   *Author*

A final view of the 1928 sequence, this time looking towards the junction from the bridge featured above.

O. J. Morris, cty. R. C. Riley

Fairburn 2—6—4T No. 42102
taking the line to Oxted on 23rd
July 1955.   *R. C. Riley*

No. 80068 with the 7.36 a.m.
train from Eastbourne to Tunbridge Wells, seen between Groombridge Junction and the station
on 11th June 1965. *John Scrace*

This picture, looking across the inclined deck of the bridge featured on page 117, is typical of many secluded, almost forgotten lineside locations.

Author's Collection

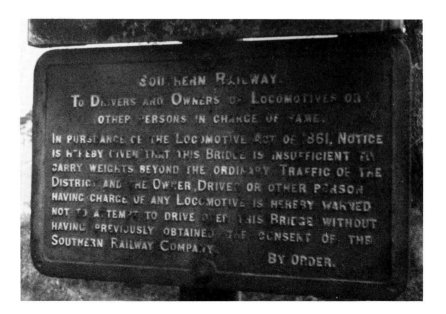

The approach road to Groombridge station in the early years of the century.

Another early view of the station forecourt, showing the ornate canopy valance which survived much longer than the similar one at Tunbridge Wells.

GROOMBRIDGE

Direct train services between Oxted and Tunbridge Wells came to an end on 5th January 1969 with the closure of the Ashurst to Groombridge spur and from that date the only trains to serve Groombridge were those operating between Tonbridge and Uckfield. Before the closure of the lines from East Grinstead and Eastbourne four years earlier, however, there were four converging routes to Tunbridge Wells which passed through Groombridge, making it a remarkably busy station for the small village it served. Well over a hundred passenger trains were handled each weekday during most of the existence of the station.

Groombridge was opened in 1866 when the branch from Three Bridges to East Grinstead was extended to Tunbridge Wells and its importance began two years later when the line from Uckfield was completed. Both of these lines were single and as they converged near Groombridge they provided another example of double single track for the last half a mile or so into the station. The earliest edition of the 25 inch Ordnance Survey map shows that there were three platform faces and the track layout suggests that the line from East Grinstead doubled as it entered the station to use the main platform for down trains and one side of the island platform for up trains. The line from Uckfield used the other side of the island before merging with the double track to Tunbridge Wells. The part of the line between Groombridge and Eridge was not doubled until 1980 when the line to Eastbourne was completed. In 1888 Groombridge

Junction to Ashurst Junction was doubled for the opening of the line to Oxted and at the same time a crossover, together with its associated signalling equipment, was installed at the western end of the station at an estimated cost of £200. Whether this included the cost of Groombridge West signal box, which opened in that year, is not clear.

The railway crossed a footpath at the junction and because the lines were in quite a deep cutting steps were provided down the embankment on each side in order to allow the right of way to continue. With the increasing traffic, this was obviously a dangerous practice and towards the end of 1889 it was agreed that a footbridge should be provided. It was possible for this to be done cheaply by making use of a bridge which was no longer required at Battersea Wharf[2] and the resulting structure was, and still is, quite a curiosity as the illustrations show. The span is some six feet below the top of the embankment with steps, possibly part of the original steps, leading down to it.

With the continuing growth of traffic and the introduction of through carriages between London and the coast being transferred at this station, further improvements were necessary. In the fifteen years following the opening of the line from Oxted a considerable amount of work was put in hand including the lengthening of the island platform and the re-alignment of the track around it. Although that work was begun in 1899 the loop was not brought back into use until about 1907 and it is doubtful if the cost was ever really justified. With the changed role of the station after 1914, when Eridge began to assume the responsibility for

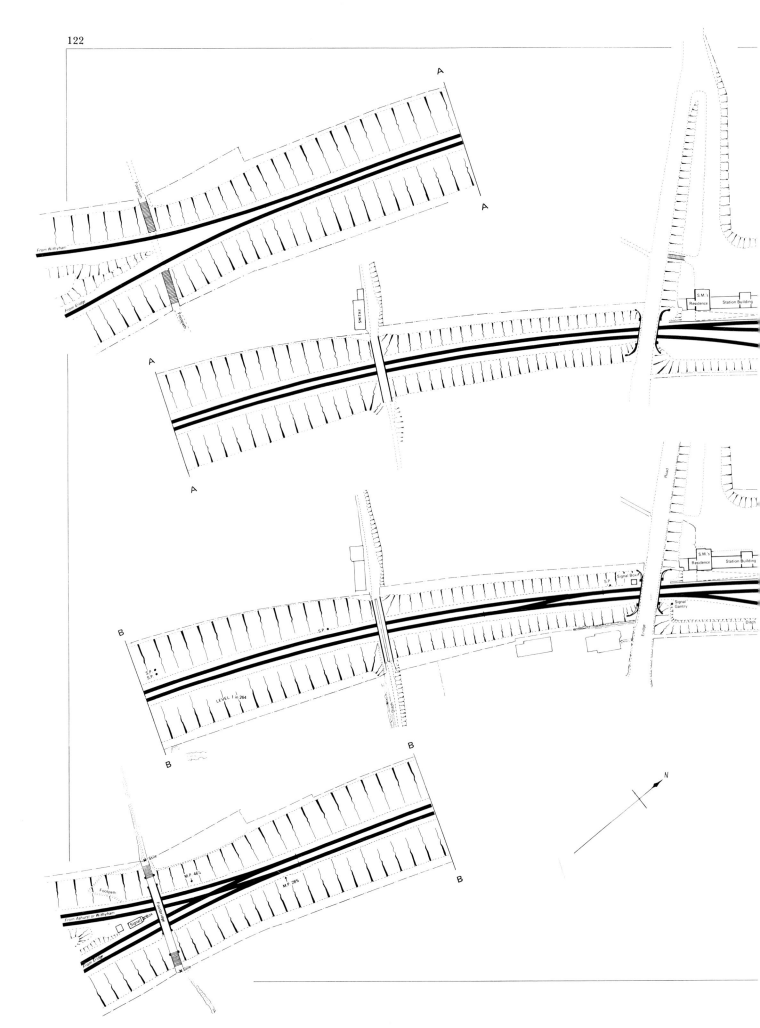

A

A
A

From Withyham

Footpath

From Eridge

Footpath

A

A

SMITHY

S.M.
Residence   Station Building

B

S.P.

S.P.
S.P.

LEVEL 1 in 264

B
B

Residence   Station Building

S.P.
S.P.   Signal Box

Signal
Gantry

Road

Ditch

Bridge

B
B

Stile

Footpath

M.P. 46¾

M.P. 28¾

From Ashurst or Withyham

Footbridge

Signal Box

From Eridge

Stile

N

GROOMBRIDGE 1874

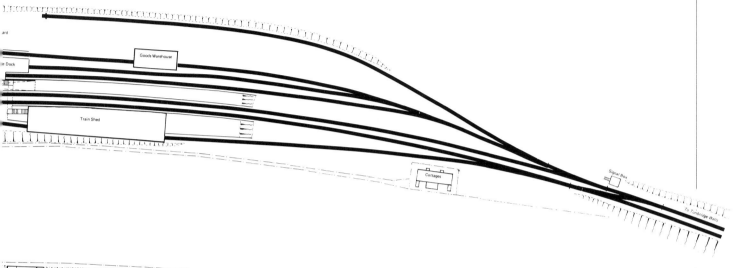

Goods Warehouse

Train Shed

Dock

ard

Goods Warehouse

Cottages

Signal Box

To Tunbridge Wells

GROOMBRIDGE 1909

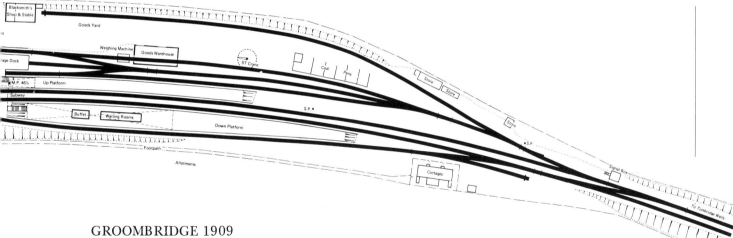

Blacksmith's
Shop & Stable

Goods Yard

Weighing Machine

Goods Warehouse

5T Crane

Coal
Pens

Store

Store

Store

age Dock

M.P. 46½

Up Platform

Subway

S.P.

Buffer

Waiting Rooms

Down Platform

S.P.

Footpath

Allotments

Cottages

Signal Box

To Tunbridge Wells

'B4' class 4–4–0 No. 2058 entering Groombridge with a Brighton to Tonbridge train. Brighton rostered a 'B4' for this route when the last 'Gladstone', No. 172, was withdrawn in 1933. Prior to their withdrawal in August 1936, Nos. 2058 and 2057 were at Eastbourne and regularly worked the Heathfield line. The distant signals, which give advance warning for Groombridge Junction, were soon to be replaced by a bracket signal.

Lens of Sutton

through carriages, there soon came a time when the loop was seldom, if ever, required. In any case, involving a reversal of direction, as it did, the transfer of through carriages at Groombridge could never have been a convenient business.

The station building, which has survived almost intact on the down platform, is an interesting and attractive structure. Built of red brick with string courses of blue and white brick, and coloured brick reveals to the doors and windows, it is similar in many ways to the much larger building of the same period at Tunbridge Wells. The stationmaster's residence is at one end of the building, adjacent to the former booking hall. In 1899 this was converted to become his office and the general waiting room was altered to allow for a new booking hall. At the same time a new goods and parcels office was added at the other end of the building, adjoining the gentlemen's toilets.[3] A subway provided access to the other platform which, according to early plans, was protected by a train shed. It seems that there was no other shelter for passengers for on 3rd March 1896 the Engineering Committee considered a letter from a Mr. H. Stewart who was urging that waiting room accommodation should be provided. Mr. Morgan was instructed to report on the best means of doing so[4] and in August he submitted plans for the proposed improvement at an estimated cost of £2,300.[5] The work was ordered to be carried out and in the following April a Form of Tender was submitted by Messrs. Richard Cook & Sons of Crawley. This was accepted on 26th May 1897.[6] The estimate was summarised as follows:

General Notes & Preliminary Items, pulling down etc.	£ 66	15	0
Excavation, Bricklayer & Drainage	£564	16	9
Mason, Slater & Slate Mason	£384	0	9
Carpenter, Joiner & Ironmonger	£370	18	3
Founder & Smith	£110	13	7
Plasterer	£ 33	9	8
Plumber & Zinc Worker	£331	4	2

Glazier	£ 42	13	7
Painter	£ 73	15	5
Surveyor's charges @ 2½%	£ 49	9	2
	£2027	16	4

Credit value of old materials from pulling down existing roof and supporting wall	£40	0	0		
Credit value of old bricks from pulling down existing platform walls	£50	0	0	£ 90	0 0
				£1937	16 4[7]

The proposed refreshment room on the island platform was the subject of a separate contract and this also went to Mr. Cook. When completed it was to be let to a Mr. Bradford at an annual rent of £10 and the solicitors were instructed to apply for a licence for the sale of intoxicating liquor therein.[8]

Following an inspection in August 1899, it was considered necessary for the down platform roof to be renewed. Messrs. R. Cook & Son's tender to carry out the work for £639 was accepted and the account for £636 10s 5d, a saving of £2 9s 7d, was settled on 5th December 1900.[9]

Even in the early days the goods yard was quite extensive and the facilities were generous, but a study of the timetable suggests that the goods traffic was fairly sparse for many of the goods trains only stopped if required. It was used as a collection point for empty wagons, however, and during one period, in Southern Railway days, it was used as a sort of holding yard for Tunbridge Wells bound trains. The early goods from Norwood Yard was left at Groombridge to be attached to the up goods from Eastbourne later in the day. The Norwood engine went on, light, to Tunbridge Wells. Included in the facilities was a brick-built goods warehouse which was equipped with a one-ton crane and there was a five-ton crane in the yard. Most unusually, a 14 ft long wagon weighbridge of twenty tons capacity was provided just outside the goods shed. There were two carriage docks

Looking through the station towards Tunbridge Wells in March 1948.

L & GRP, cty. David & Charles

The rail-built bracket signal shown in these views dated from about 1938.

D. Clayton

'E4' class 0—6—2 tank No. 2580 at the head of an Eastbourne to Tunbridge Wells train. The date of this photograph is uncertain but the white bands on the canopy support columns suggest the 1940s.

Lens of Sutton

Groombridge in 1951. The West box, which was reduced to ground frame status in 1907 and closed in 1958, may just be seen through the bridge. This small timber-built box was only nine feet square, with a floor height of nine inches. It contained thirteen levers.   *D. Clayton*

The original signal box at the east end of the station.

with end-loading facilities and the provision of cattle pens complete with a supply of water was authorised in 1889.[10] In the same year it was decided to provide a blacksmith's shop for the use of the Permanent Way Department in the Tunbridge Wells District and this still survives and may be seen just inside the yard entrance. A pair of cottages was built during the following year, one of which was for the company blacksmith. The other cottage was for the ticket collector.[11] There were crossovers between three of the sidings giving an apparent run-round facility which was rare outside the larger yards. Probably the reason for this provision was the easier release of wagons such as cattle vans which may have been trapped at the inner end of a siding and perhaps compensate for the absence of a head-shunt which must have created problems for the shunter.

There was some very interesting signalling at the station but the photographs and diagrams illustrate this far more clearly than any number of words. The original signal box at the east end of the station probably dates from 1866 and was one of the longest surviving 'Brighton' boxes, although it had lost some of its original appearance. A double set of windows gave the box an unusually tall look but the purpose of the upper set is not known and for many years the glazing was obscured by paint. Groombridge Junction box was provided in time for the opening of the line from Eastbourne in 1880 and a third box, Groombridge West, was provided with the completion of the line from Oxted in 1888. The original box now became known as Groombridge East but Groombridge West was little more than a ground frame, being only 9 ft square and at ground level, and in 1907 it was indeed reduced to that status. The original box then reverted to its original title of Groombridge. All three boxes were closed on 23rd November

The goods yard was largely disused by 1969. The small cattle dock survives on the left. *Author*

The goods warehouse still survives and, in 1971, so did the coal pens and loading gauge. *Author*

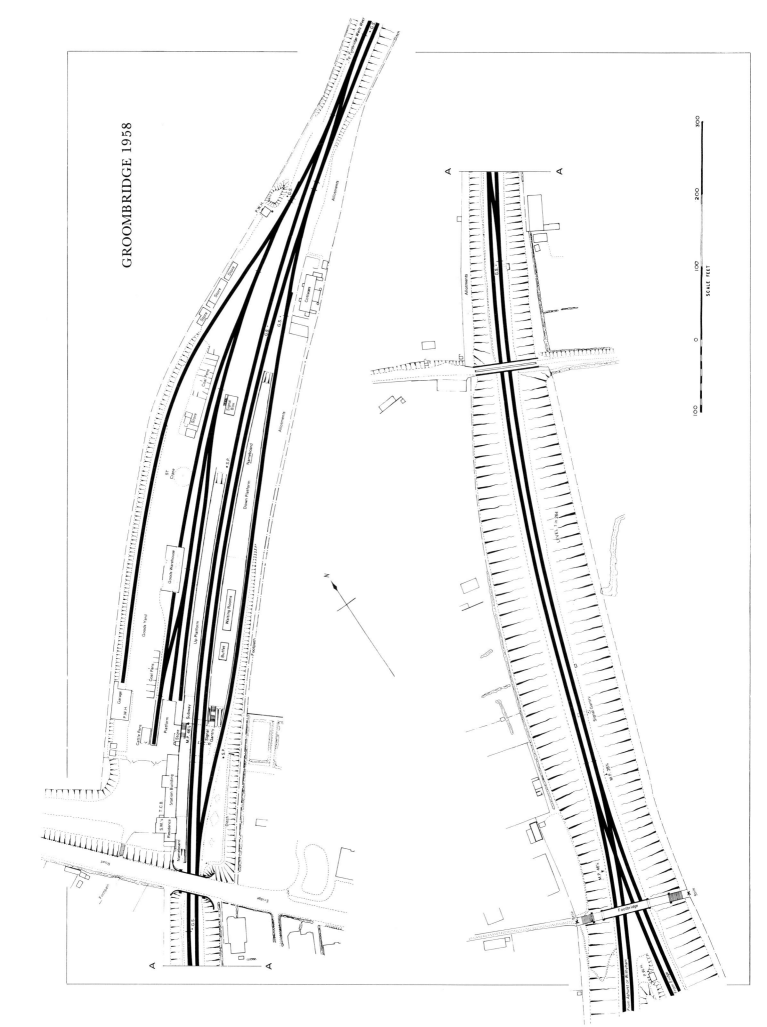

GROOMBRIDGE 1958

SCALE FEET

300 200 100 0 100

Compared with earlier views, apart from the renewal of the valance, little else had changed by 1969.   *John Minnis Collection*

'I3' class 4—4—2 tank No. 2048 with a Tunbridge Wells to Eastbourne train in March 1948. By this date the class was no longer considered capable of handling London trains. The pair of cottages built for the blacksmith and the ticket collector almost come into the picture on the right-hand side.

Real Photographs

130

This view, showing both old and new signal boxes, also features the pair of cottages provided in 1890 for the blacksmith and ticket collector.

Collection Brian Hart

1958, when they were replaced by a new box during resignalling. This lasted barely ten years for the box was closed on 5th January 1969, when the Groombridge to Ashurst spur closed. With no junction and a very much reduced train service not even the signals were required.

The station closed in July 1985, but the line continued to be used for working empty trains to Tunbridge Wells until 12th August, when alternative storage was provided at Selsdon.

The new signal box on 24th May 1965. *John Scrace*

1 Engineering Committee Meeting: 22. 6.1887 Minute 6
2 ,, ,, ,, 19.11.1889 Minute 10
3 ,, ,, ,, 15.1.1889 Minute 1
4 ,, ,, ,, 3.3.1896 Minute 17
5 ,, ,, ,, 5.8.1896 Minute 13
6 ,, ,, ,, 26.5.1897 Minute 3
7 From Richard Cook & Sons' Form of Tender, Contract General Conditions and Specifications and Approximate Bills of Quantities for Platform Walls, Waiting Rooms and Platform Roof at Groombridge Station. (Public Records Office, Kew)
8 Engineering Committee Meeting: 7.7.1897 Minute 10
,, ,, ,, 14.7.1897 Minute 5
9 ,, ,, ,, 22.6.1898 Minute 4
,, ,, ,, 23.8.1899 Minute 2
,, ,, ,, 25.10.1899 Minute 2
,, ,, ,, 5.12.1900 Minute 2
10 ,, ,, ,, 30.7.1889 Minute 1
11 ,, ,, ,, 19.11.1889 Minute 4

ADAM'S WELL

Adam's Well Crossing Box was between Groombridge and High Rocks Halt. It was demolished
c.1956. *John Minnis Collection & Brian Hart*

HIGH ROCKS HALT

High Rocks Halt, just three-quarters of a mile out of Tunbridge Wells was opened in 1907 for the benefit of climbers who used the nearby rocks as a training ground for more serious mountaineering activities. The platforms were staggered either side of the road bridge and a most rickety looking stairway led down to the platform for trains out of Tunbridge Wells (the down platform for East-bourne and Brighton bound trains and the up platform for London bound trains). The view above shows a down train for Brighton, headed by a 'Q' class 0—6—0 No. 30546, approaching the road bridge. *Lens of Sutton*

'H' class 0—4—4T No. 31310 at Tunbridge Wells West with an Oxted push-pull on 16th March 1957.

R. C. *Riley*

TUNBRIDGE WELLS

Tunbridge Wells station during the early years of the century.   *Lens of Sutton*

'D1' class 0—4—2T No. 2253 on the 1.50 p.m. Eastbourne train (which comprised just three coaches) on 14th May 1949. This engine, the last 'D1' active in East Sussex, was withdrawn later that year.

R. C. Riley

BR standard 2—6—4T No. 80149 on Heathfield bank with the 11.10 a.m. Tonbridge to Eastbourne train on 16th June 1962.

S. C. Nash

CHAPTER SIX

CONCLUSION

IN a final bid to attract passenger traffic over the line, an hourly service of trains between Tunbridge Wells and Eastbourne was instituted in June 1956, and the standard class 4 2–6–4 tank locomotives were brought in to work the three-coach corridor sets. By 1965, when the line closed, the frequency of passenger services had actually been increased to thirteen trains in each direction during the week, and six in each direction on Sundays. In view of the way in which the goods traffic had been dissipated, however, a suspicious mind might wonder if this improved service incurred increased costs without a corresponding increase in receipts, thus creating a loss which would justify closure.

On reflection, the line's absence from any of the electrification schemes proposed either by the Southern Railway or its successor, Southern Region, could have been taken as a portent of its future. By the time the diesel multiple units were introduced it was probably too late and during the 1960s there were relatively few people who challenged the idea that the car, bus or lorry could fulfil the transport needs of a community. What challenges there were were often emotional rather than practical.

Of the thirteen trains in the up direction, four terminated at Tunbridge Wells and nine continued on to Tonbridge. In the down direction eight trains began their journey from Tonbridge, four from Tunbridge Wells and one from Eridge and the 8.20 a.m. down train from Tonbridge terminated at Polegate. In addition to these services there were still two trains in each direction working between Eastbourne and Heathfield. The goods services, however, fell off dramatically during the last few years. 1960 was the last year in which the daily goods worked through in each direction but in that year there was also a daily goods working from Polegate to Horam and return. In the up direction this train ran direct to Horam after an allowance of forty-eight minutes at Hailsham but twenty minutes were allowed at Hellingly in the down direction. In the following year the only goods working was one in the up direction which left Polegate at

DMU No. 1310, working the 9.56 a.m. from Tonbridge, departs from Mayfield on 11th June 1965.

John Scrace

The start of the diesel age with DMU No. 1304 forming the 12.45 p.m. Eastbourne to Tunbridge Wells. It is seen here leaving Heathfield Tunnel on 16th June 1962.   *S. C. Nash*

7.15 a.m. for Eridge where it was due at 11.20 a.m. and in 1964 the goods timetable was as follows:

	Arrive	Pass	Depart
Polegate			8.55 a.m.
Hailsham	9.05 a.m.		10.05 a.m.
Hellingly		10.10 a.m.	
Horam		10.19 a.m.	
Heathfield	10.30 a.m.		11.15 a.m.
Horam	11.23 a.m.		11.24 a.m.
Hellingley	11.34 a.m.		11.50 a.m.
Hailsham	11.56 a.m.		12.25 p.m.
Polegate	12.34 p.m.		

There were a number of 'last trains' to mark the occasion of the closure and, although the weekends were usually the preserve of the DMUs, it was arranged for 2—6—4 tank No. 80144 to work the 2.47 p.m. from Eastbourne and the 6.00 p.m. return from Tunbridge Wells on Saturday, 12th June, to provide the last steam-hauled service. The last steam-hauled train to use the line was on the Sunday and this was the 'Wealdsman Rail Tour' organised by the Locomotive Club of Great Britain. U class 2—6—0 No. 31803 and N class 2—6—0 No. 31411 were the locomotives allocated for this duty. The last trains to stop at Rotherfield and Mayfield were the 7.47 p.m. from Eastbourne and the 8.29 p.m. from Eridge and at Mayfield a wreath was placed on the front of the DMU with the inscription 'Farewell Faithful Servant'. The last passenger trains on the Southern part of the line were the 9.47 p.m. from Eastbourne which returned from Heathfield at 10.24 p.m. When this train left Horam Guy Fawkes rockets were fired as well as fog detonators but it would seem that there were far more spectators than passengers and when the train arrived at Eastbourne only fifteen alighted.

From 14th June 1965 the section of the line from Hailsham to Heathfield was retained for goods traffic and worked as a siding to the following timetable:

	Tuesdays & Fridays only		*Mons, Weds & Thurs only*	
Polegate	Depart	11.15 a.m.	Depart	11.15 a.m.
Hailsham	Depart	11.25 a.m.	Arrive	11.25 p.m.
Hellingly	Pass			
Horam	Pass			
Heathfield	Arrive	11.50 a.m.		
Heathfield	Depart	12.15 p.m.		
Horam	Pass			
Hellingly	Pass			
Hailsham	Depart	12.35 p.m.	Depart	12.35 p.m.
Polegate	Arrive	12.45 p.m.	Arrive	12.45 p.m.

The Heathfield service was allocated to the type 3 diesel-electric locomotives but, because of the gradients, trains were restricted to twelve loaded wagons, an unspoken tribute perhaps to the old Brighton tank engines which worked the line for so many years. This service ceased abruptly on 26th April 1968 when a lorry damaged the road bridge at Horsebridge, just south of Hellingly, closing the line until further notice. As the line was scheduled for complete closure from 6th May it never re-opened.

'D6572' near Hailsham with the 5.20 p.m. Hailsham-Polegate on 11th June 1965.   *John Scrace*

Plans to withdraw the services between Polegate and Hailsham were announced in October 1967 and, in spite of strong objections, the goods service was withdrawn on 2nd August 1968. Five weeks later, on 8th September, the passenger services came to an end even though, according to a document published by the Transport Users' Consultative Committee, British Railways agreed that Hailsham was a growing town and that buses would mean longer and more expensive journeys and would not be able to cater for the needs of cyclists or mothers with prams and the like. Apparently it felt that only a small proportion of the thousands of new residents were likely to use a train service and the line closed.

The last passenger train left Hailsham for Polegate and Eastbourne on Sunday, 8th September, at 10.30 p.m. which, by strange coincidence, was the same time that the last train left Hailsham for Brighton on that opening day in 1849. This train, which had arrived from Eastbourne ten minutes earlier, was composed of two diesel multiple units of two and three coaches coupled together to provide extra accommodation for some one hundred and fifty passengers who were travelling on the last trains. A considerable number of people were on the platform at Hailsham to witness the departure of the train which moved out slowly to the accompaniment of detonator explosions and the sounding of the two-tone horn to the musical timing of 'Auld Lang Syne'. All along the line between Hailsham and Polegate, keepers and their families at the three level crossings and inhabitants from houses near the line waved their farewell as the train passed by with its horn sounding continuously. Further detonators were exploded by the train as it left Polegate for Eastbourne and the last remnant of the 'Cuckoo Line' faded into history.

MAP OF THE LINE

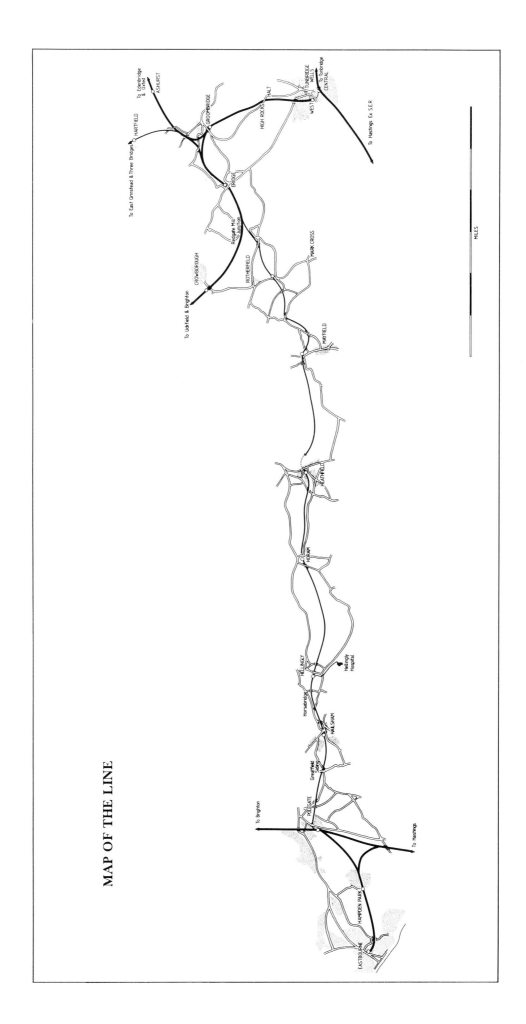

MILES

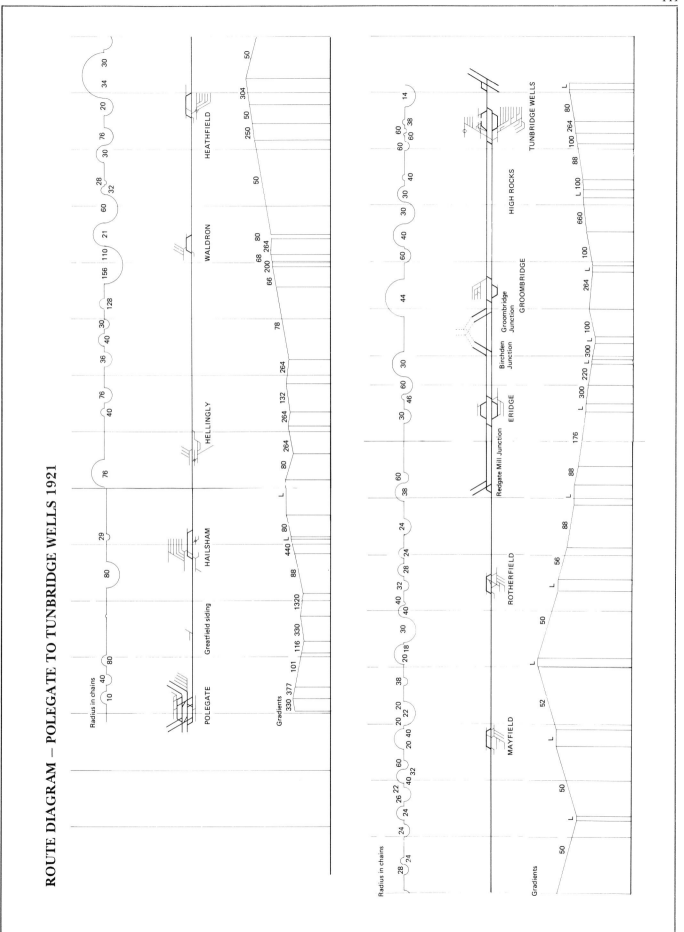

ROUTE DIAGRAM – POLEGATE TO TUNBRIDGE WELLS 1921

142

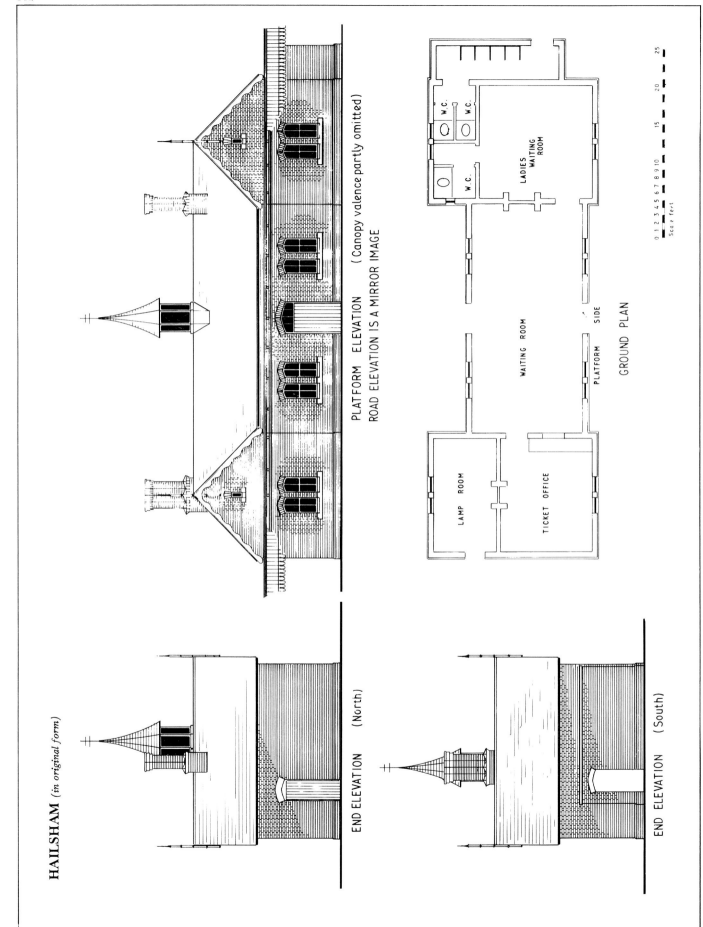

HAILSHAM *(in original form)*

END ELEVATION (North)

END ELEVATION (South)

PLATFORM ELEVATION (Canopy valence partly omitted)
ROAD ELEVATION IS A MIRROR IMAGE

GROUND PLAN

LAMP ROOM

TICKET OFFICE

WAITING ROOM

PLATFORM SIDE

LADIES WAITING ROOM

W.C.

W.C.

W.C.

0 1 2 3 4 5 6 7 8 9 10   15   20   25
Scale feet

HAILSHAM UP PLATFORM WAITING ROOM

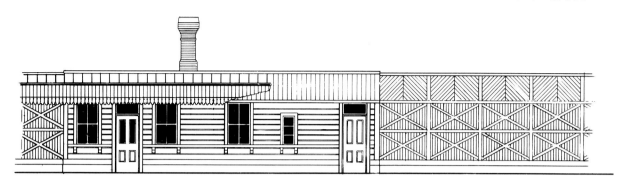

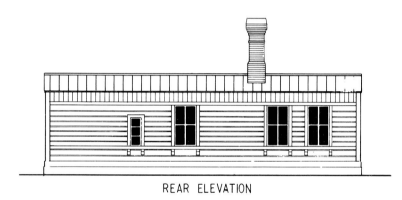

REAR ELEVATION

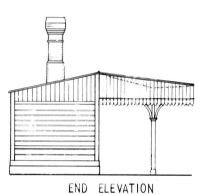

END ELEVATION

0 1 2 3 4 5 6 7 8 9 10   15   20   25
Scale feet

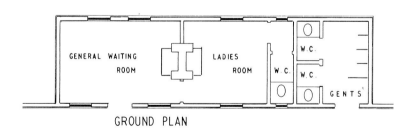

GENERAL WAITING ROOM   LADIES ROOM   W.C.   W.C.   W.C.   GENTS

GROUND PLAN

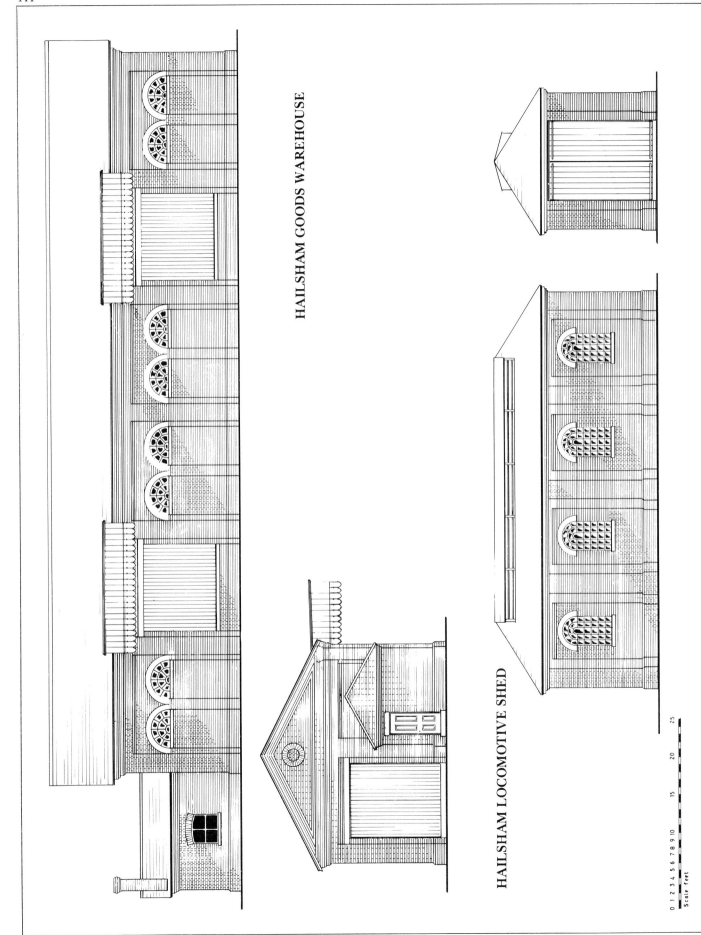

HAILSHAM GOODS WAREHOUSE

HAILSHAM LOCOMOTIVE SHED

0 1 2 3 4 5 6 7 8 9 10   15   20   25
Scale Feet

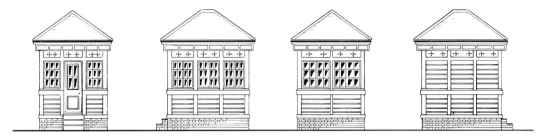

SMALL SIGNAL BOX DIMENSIONS

HAILSHAM	13'6"x 9'6"	Floor height	4'8"
HELLINGLY	11'6"x 9'6"	~ ~	5'0"
WALDRON	11'6"x 9'6"	~ ~	4'6"
HEATHFIELD	11'6"x 9'6"	~ ~	5'0"
MAYFIELD	13'6"x 9'6"	~ ~	5'0"
ROTHERFIELD	13'6" 9'6"	~ ~	5'6"

SIGNAL BOX STYLES FOUND ON CUCKOO LINE

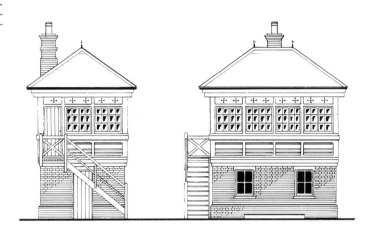

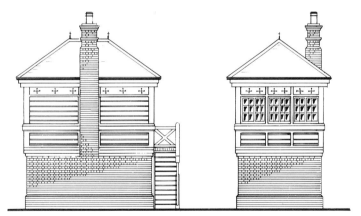

LARGE SIGNAL BOX DIMENSIONS:

HAILSHAM	17'6"x 11'6"	Floor height	8'0"
HELLINGLY	~ ~ ~ ~	~ ~	~ ~
WALDRON	16'6"x 11'6"	~ ~	8'0"
HEATHFIELD	18'6"x 12'6"	~ ~	8'6"
MAYFIELD	18'6"x 11'6"	~ ~	12'8"
ROTHERFIELD	18'6"x 11'6"	~ ~	8'4"

HELLINGLY (*Horeham Road similar*)

No screen wall at HOREHAM ROAD

See ROAD ELEVATION for tile pattern at HOREHAM ROAD

Dotted line shows outline of wall at HOREHAM ROAD

PLATFORM ELEVATION

← IN THIS SECTION →

Original drawings indicate identical layout to that at ROTHERFIELD

Internal details differed at HOREHAM ROAD

GROUND PLAN (Before 1905)

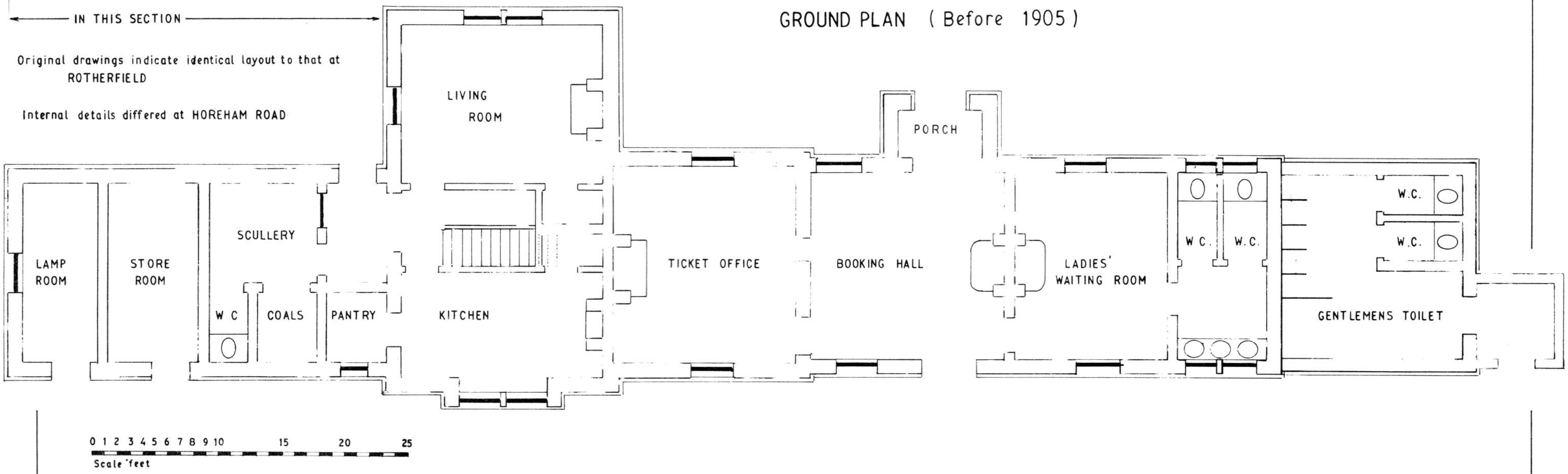

W.C.

W.C.

GENTLEMENS TOILET

W.C.

W.C.

LADIES' WAITING ROOM

PORCH

BOOKING HALL

TICKET OFFICE

LIVING ROOM

KITCHEN

PANTRY

SCULLERY

COALS

W C

STORE ROOM

LAMP ROOM

0 1 2 3 4 5 6 7 8 9 10   15   20   25

Scale 'feet

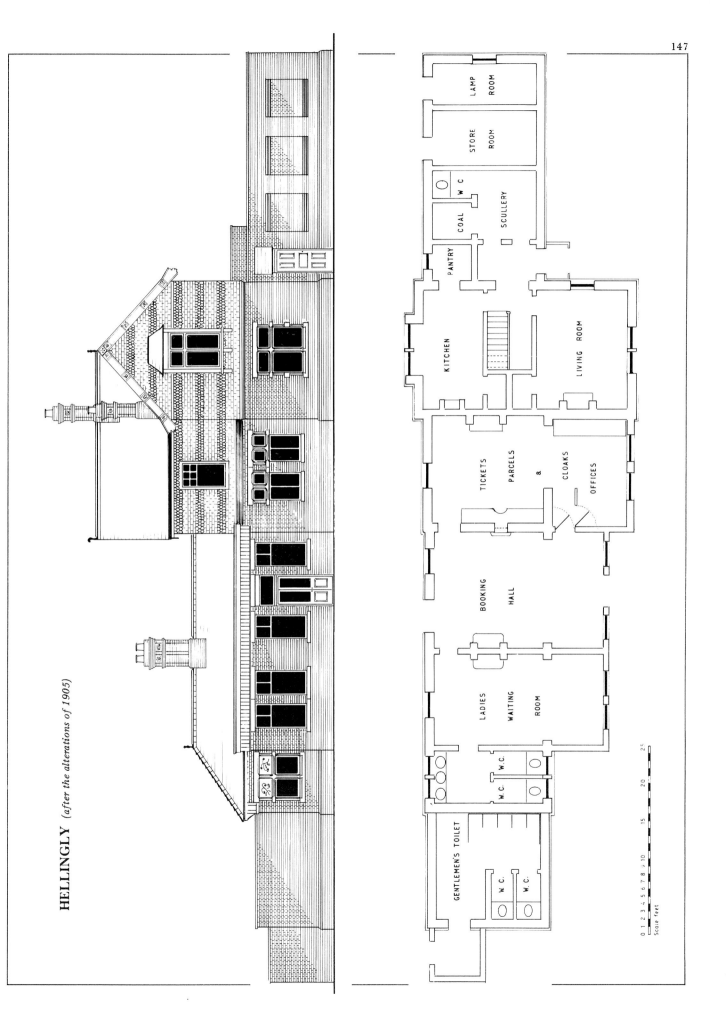

HELLINGLY *(after the alterations of 1905)*

LAMP ROOM

STORE ROOM

PANTRY

COAL

W C

SCULLERY

KITCHEN

LIVING ROOM

TICKETS

PARCELS

&

CLOAKS

OFFICES

BOOKING HALL

LADIES WAITING ROOM

W.C.

W.C.

GENTLEMEN'S TOILET

W.C.

W.C.

0 1 2 3 4 5 6 7 8 9 10   15   20   25

Scale feet

WALDRON & HOREHAM ROAD

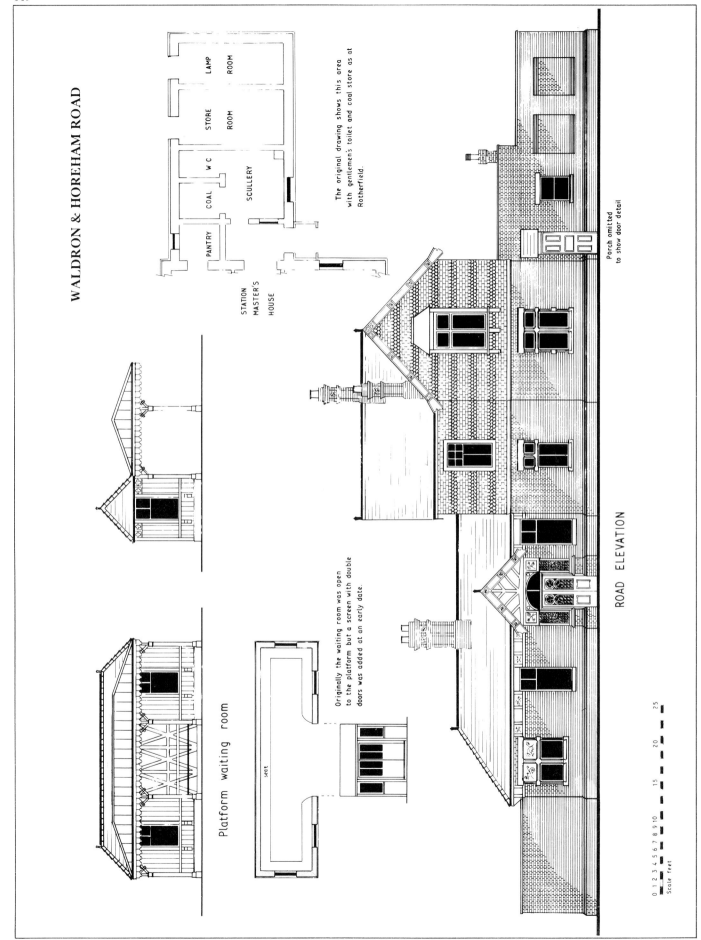

PANTRY

COAL

W C

STORE
ROOM

LAMP
ROOM

SCULLERY

STATION
MASTER'S
HOUSE

The original drawing shows this area
with gentlemen's toilet and coal store as at
Rotherfield.

Platform waiting room

seat

Originally the waiting room was open
to the platform but a screen with double
doors was added at an early date.

ROAD ELEVATION

Porch omitted
to show door detail

0 1 2 3 4 5 6 7 8 9 10   15   20   25

Scale feet

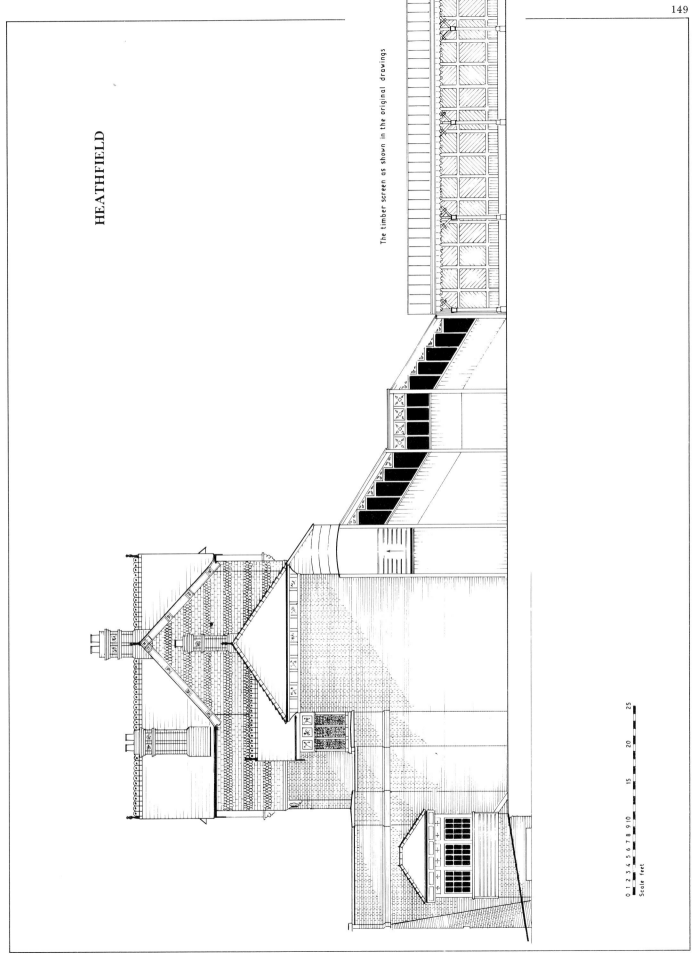

HEATHFIELD

The timber screen as shown in the original drawings

0 1 2 3 4 5 6 7 8 9 10   15   20   25
Scale feet

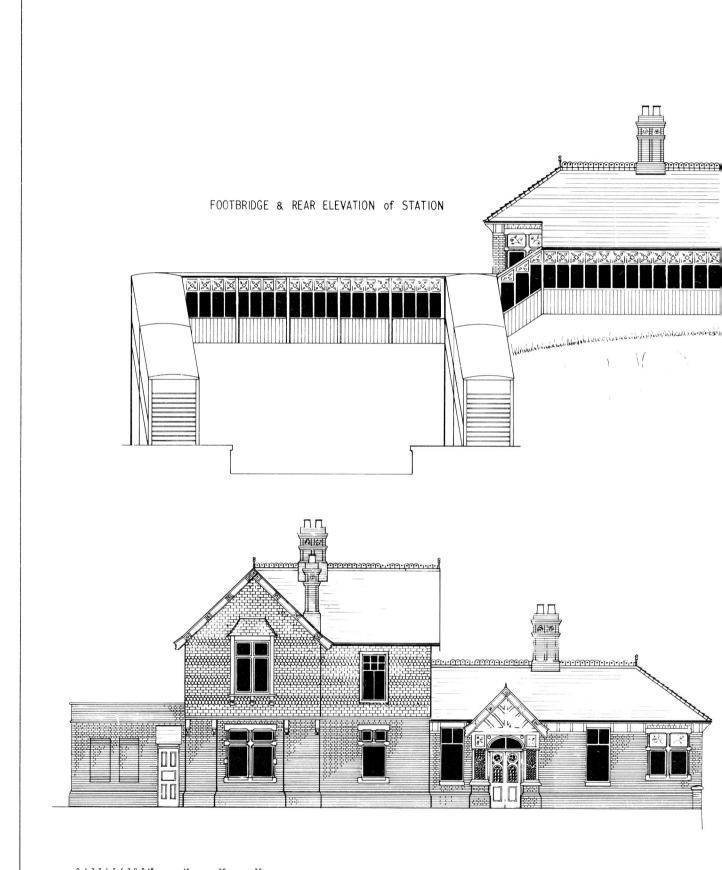

FOOTBRIDGE & REAR ELEVATION of STATION

0 1 2 3 4 5 6 7 8 9 10   15   20   25

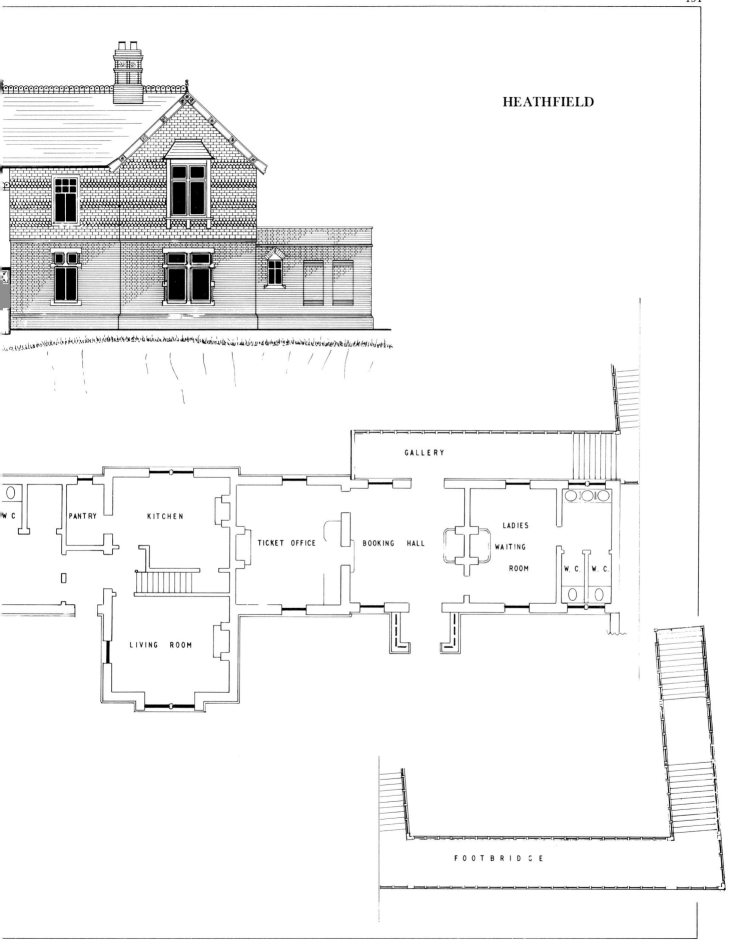

HEATHFIELD

GALLERY

W C   PANTRY   KITCHEN

TICKET OFFICE   BOOKING   HALL

LADIES

WAITING

ROOM

W. C.   W. C.

LIVING   ROOM

FOOTBRIDGE

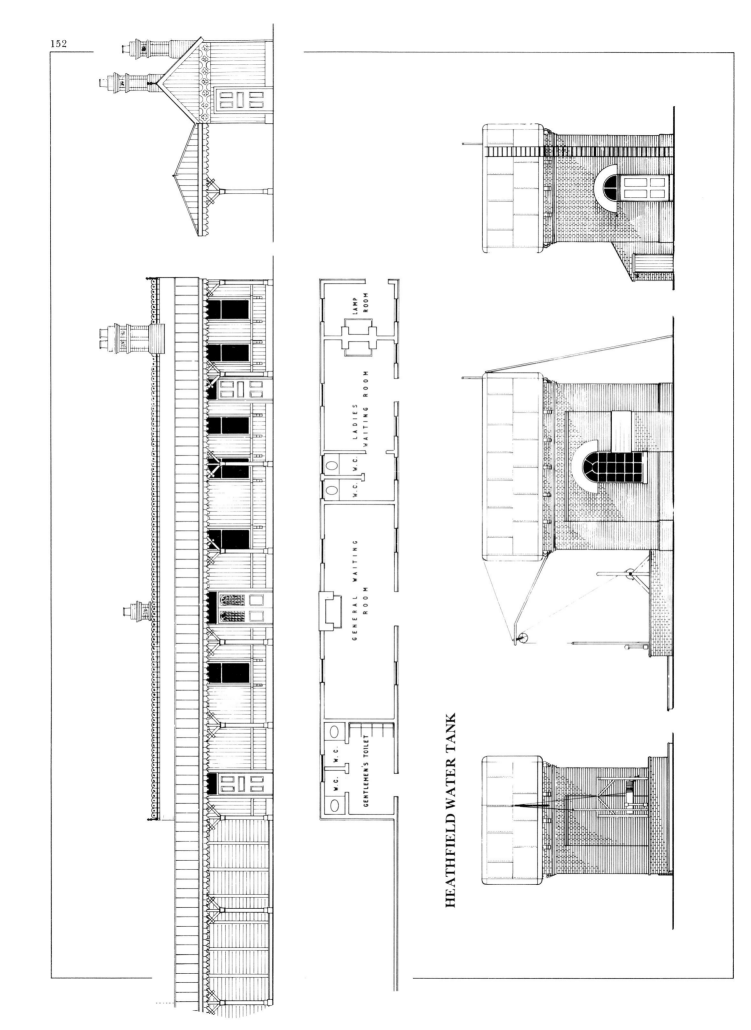

LAMP ROOM

LADIES WAITING ROOM

W.C. W.C.

GENERAL WAITING ROOM

W.C. W.C.

GENTLEMEN'S TOILET

HEATHFIELD WATER TANK

GOODS WAREHOUSES AT HEATHFIELD, MAYFIELD & ROTHERFIELD

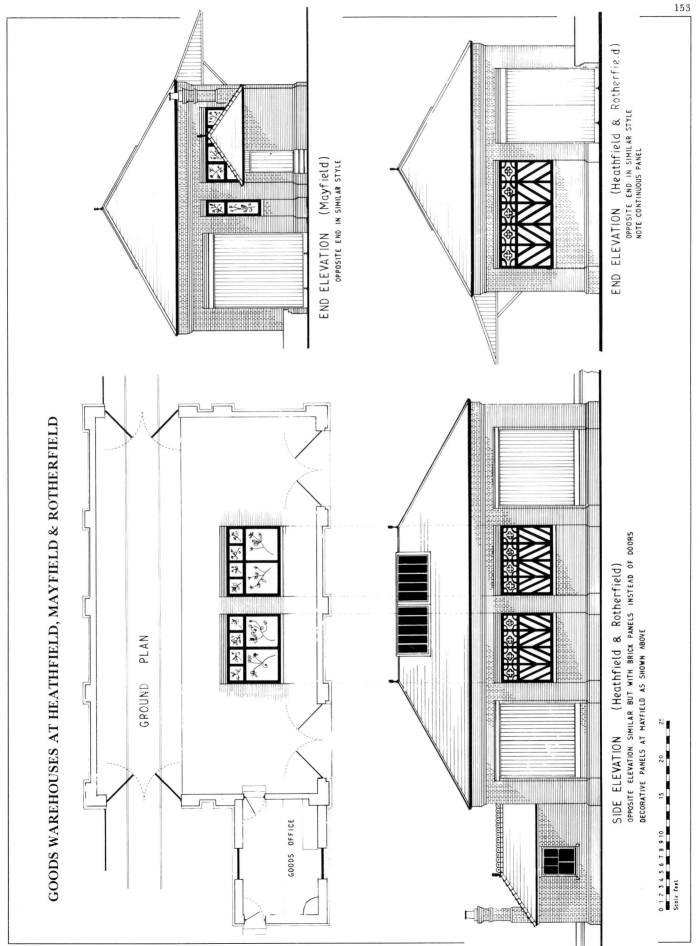

GROUND PLAN

GOODS OFFICE

GOODS

END ELEVATION (Mayfield)
OPPOSITE END IN SIMILAR STYLE

END ELEVATION (Heathfield & Rotherfield)
OPPOSITE END IN SIMILAR STYLE
NOTE CONTINUOUS PANEL

SIDE ELEVATION (Heathfield & Rotherfield)
OPPOSITE ELEVATION SIMILAR BUT WITH BRICK PANELS INSTEAD OF DOORS
DECORATIVE PANELS AT MAYFIELD AS SHOWN ABOVE

0 1 2 3 4 5 6 7 8 9 10   15   20   25
Scale feet

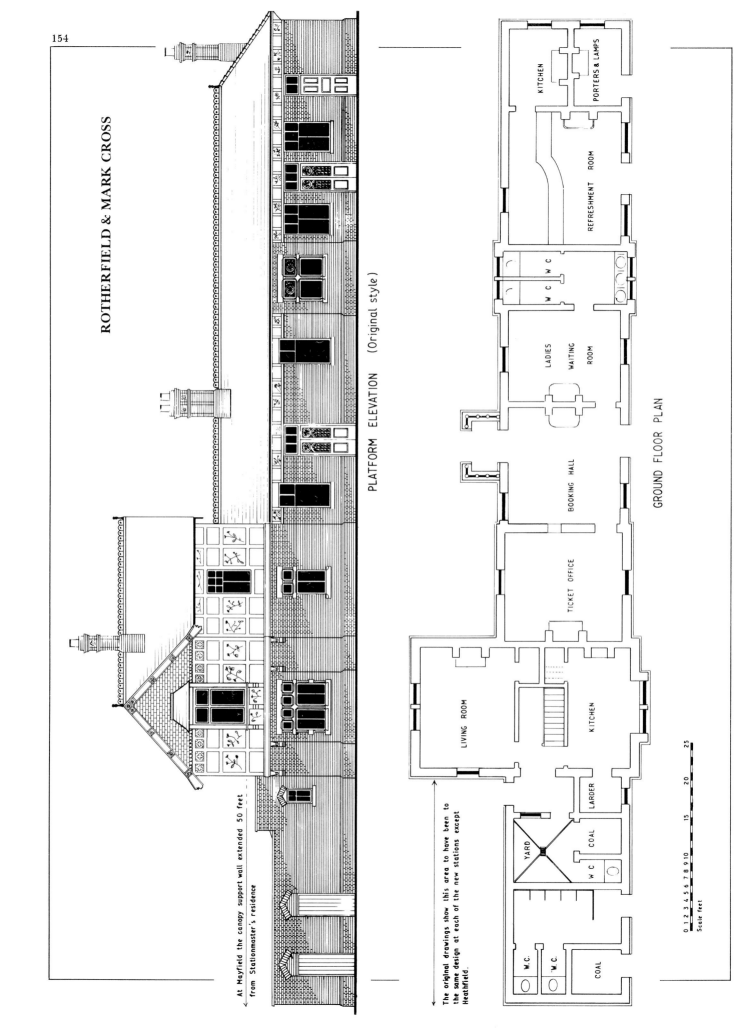

154

ROTHERFIELD & MARK CROSS

PLATFORM ELEVATION (Original style)

At Mayfield the canopy support wall extended 50 feet from Stationmaster's residence

The original drawings show this area to have been to the same design at each of the new stations except Heathfield.

GROUND FLOOR PLAN

KITCHEN

PORTERS & LAMPS

REFRESHMENT ROOM

W C

W C

W C

LADIES WAITING ROOM

BOOKING HALL

TICKET OFFICE

LIVING ROOM

KITCHEN

LARDER

COAL

YARD

W.C.

COAL

W.C.

W.C.

0 1 2 3 4 5 6 7 8 9 10   15   20   25

Scale feet

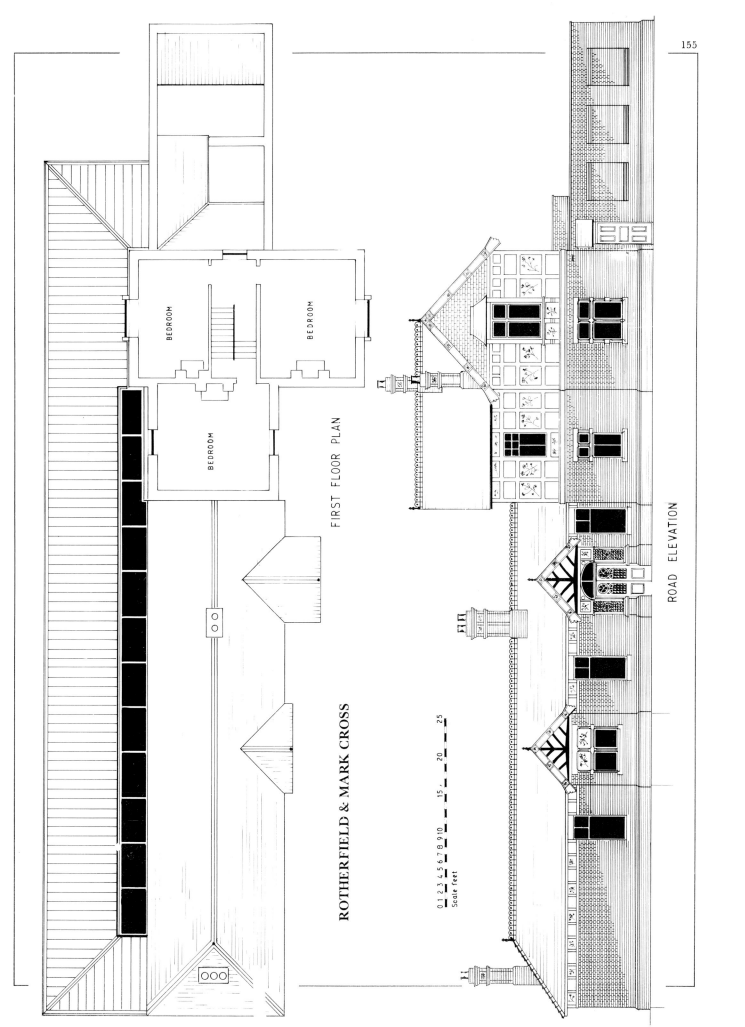

ROTHERFIELD & MARK CROSS

FIRST FLOOR PLAN

BEDROOM

BEDROOM

BEDROOM

0 1 2 3 4 5 6 7 8 9 10   15   20   25
Scale feet

ROAD ELEVATION

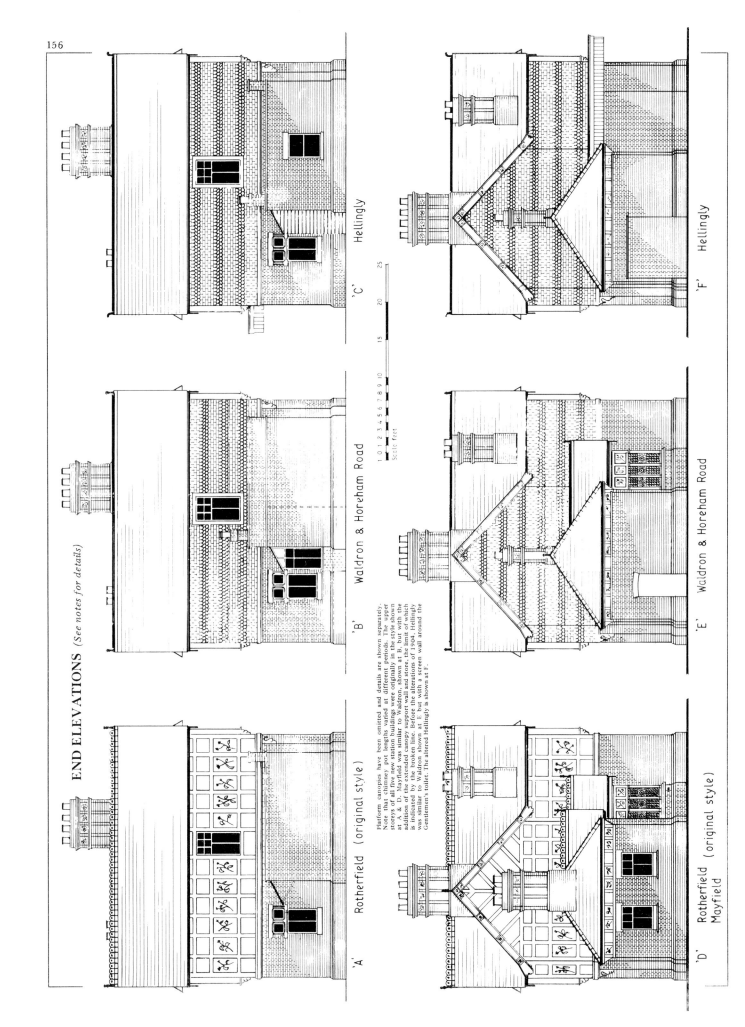

END ELEVATIONS *(See notes for details)*

'A' Rotherfield (original style)

'B' Waldron & Horeham Road

'C' Hellingly

'D' Rotherfield (original style)
Mayfield

'E' Waldron & Horeham Road

'F' Hellingly

1 0 1 2 3 4 5 6 7 8 9 10   15   20   25
Scale feet

Platform canopies have been omitted and details are shown separately. Note that chimney pot lengths varied at different periods. The upper storeys of all five new station buildings were originally in the style shown at A & D. Mayfield was similar to Waldron, shown at B, but with the addition of the extended canopy support wall and store, the limit of which is indicated by the broken line. Before the alterations of 1904, Hellingly was similar to Waldron shown at E but with a screen wall around the Gentlemen's toilet. The altered Hellingly is shown at F.

157

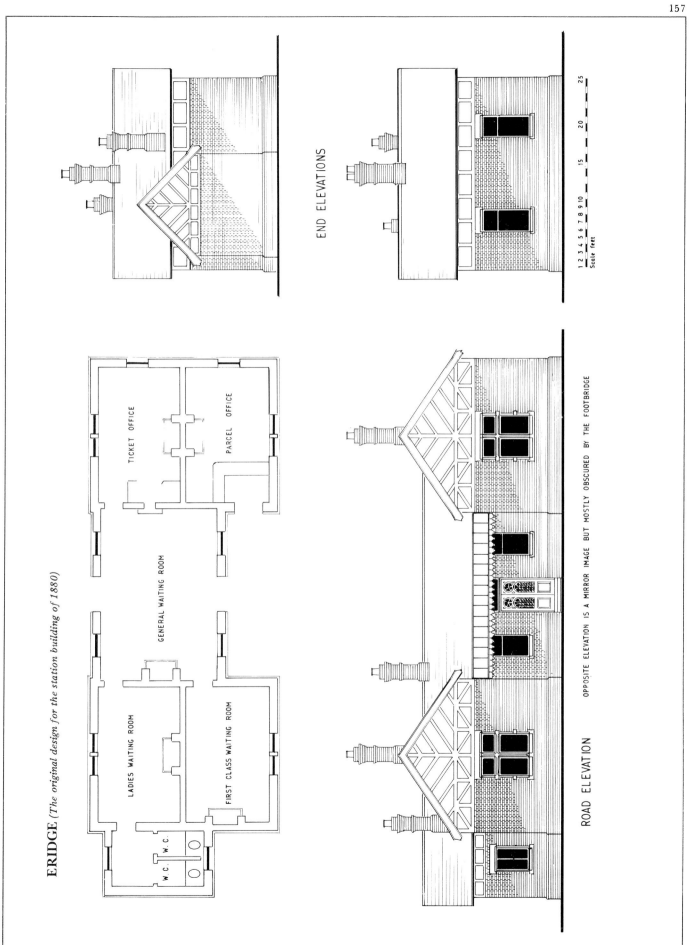

ERIDGE *(The original design for the station building of 1880)*

TICKET OFFICE

PARCEL OFFICE

LADIES WAITING ROOM

GENERAL WAITING ROOM

FIRST CLASS WAITING ROOM

W.C. W.C. W.C.

END ELEVATIONS

1 2 3 4 5 6 7 8 9 10   15   20   25
Scale feet

ROAD ELEVATION   OPPOSITE ELEVATION IS A MIRROR IMAGE BUT MOSTLY OBSCURED BY THE FOOTBRIDGE

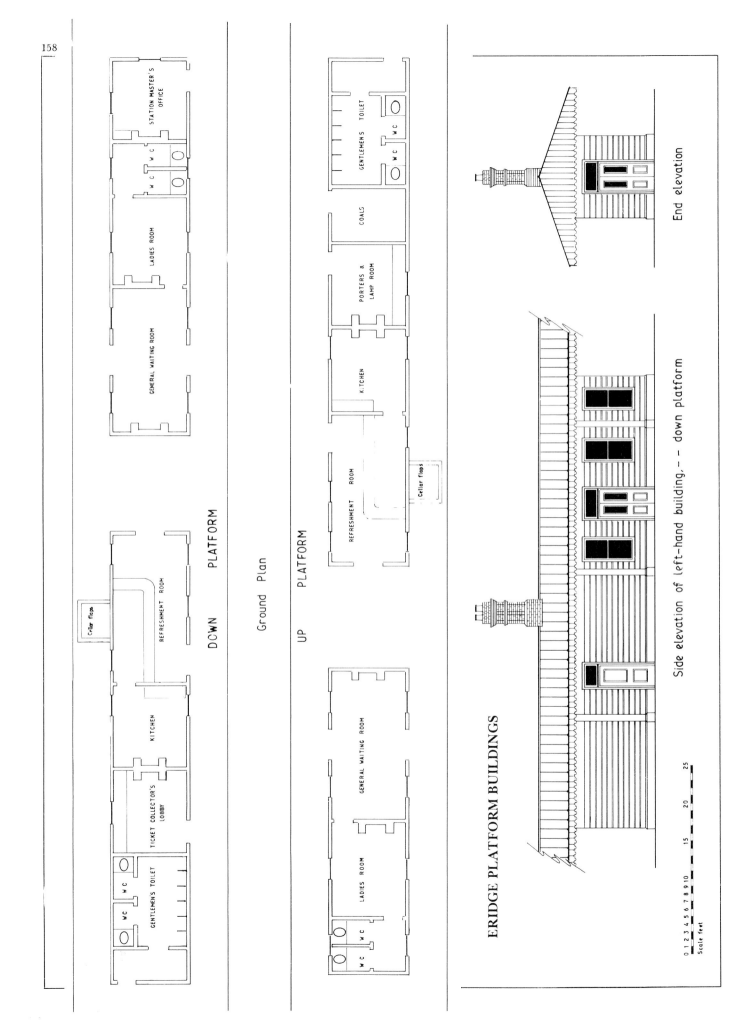

STATION MASTER'S OFFICE

LADIES ROOM

W C W C

GENERAL WAITING ROOM

Cellar flaps

REFRESHMENT ROOM

KITCHEN

TICKET COLLECTOR'S LOBBY

GENTLEMEN'S TOILET

W C W C

DOWN PLATFORM

GENTLEMEN'S TOILET

W C W C

COALS

PORTERS & LAMP ROOM

K.TCHEN

REFRESHMENT ROOM

Cellar flaps

GENERAL WAITING ROOM

LADIES ROOM

W C W C

UP PLATFORM

Ground Plan

End elevation

Side elevation of left-hand building,- - down platform

ERIDGE PLATFORM BUILDINGS

0 1 2 3 4 5 6 7 8 9 10   15   20   25
Scale feet

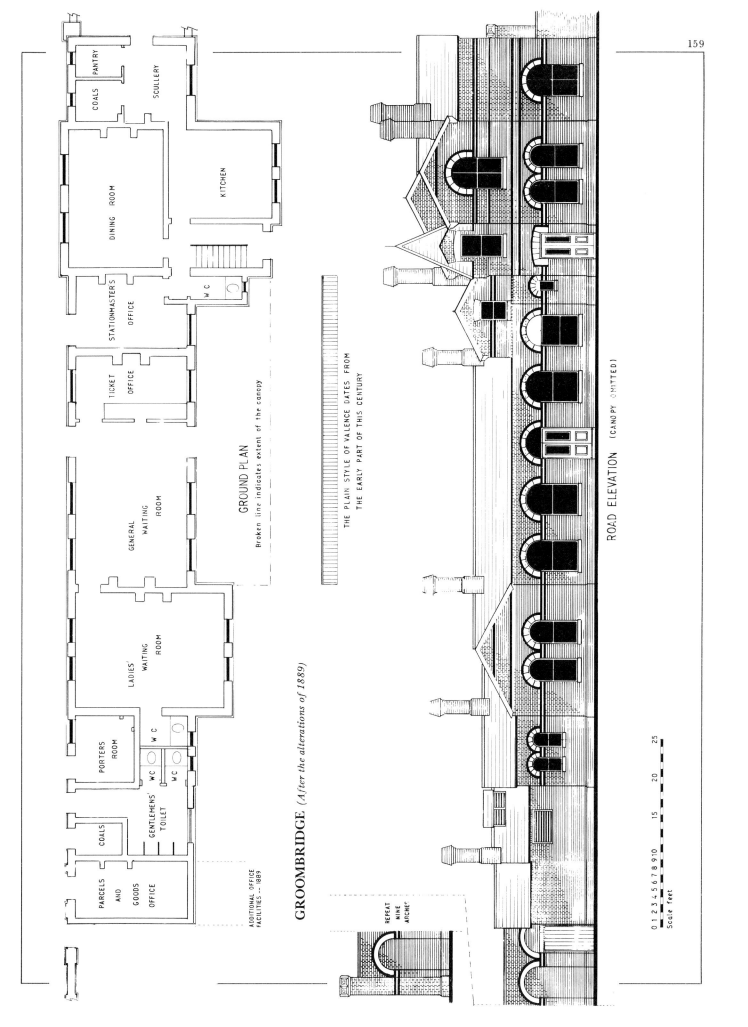

COALS
PANTRY
SCULLERY

DINING ROOM

KITCHEN

STATIONMASTER'S OFFICE

W C

TICKET OFFICE

GROUND PLAN

Broken line indicates extent of the canopy

GENERAL WAITING ROOM

LADIES' WAITING ROOM

PORTERS ROOM

W C

GENTLEMENS' TOILET

W C

W C

PARCELS AND GOODS OFFICE

COALS

ADDITIONAL OFFICE FACILITIES — 1889

GROOMBRIDGE *(After the alterations of 1889)*

THE PLAIN STYLE OF VALENCE DATES FROM THE EARLY PART OF THIS CENTURY

REPEAT NINE ARCHES

ROAD ELEVATION (CANOPY OMITTED)

0 1 2 3 4 5 6 7 8 9 10   15   20   25
Scale feet

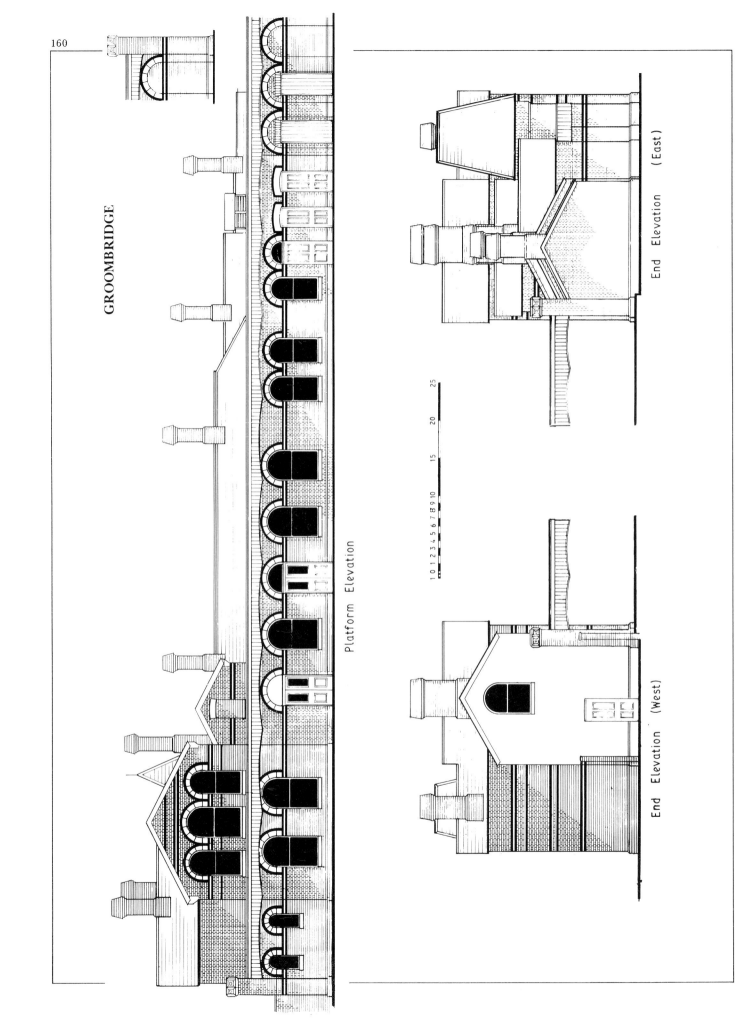

GROOMBRIDGE

Platform Elevation

End Elevation (East)

End Elevation (West)

0 1 2 3 4 5 6 7 8 9 10   15   20   25

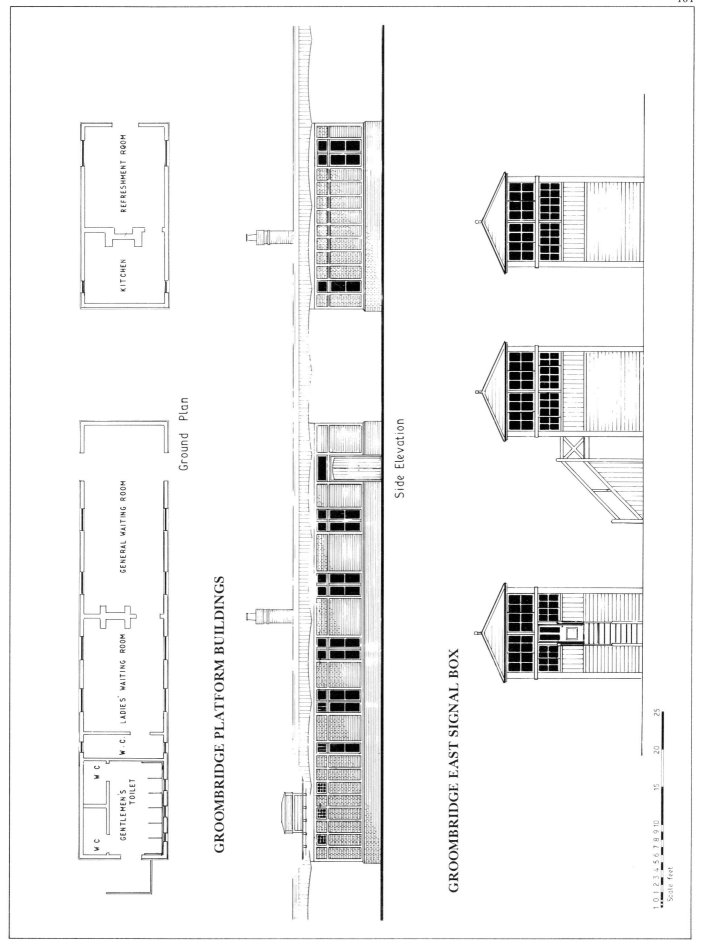

GROOMBRIDGE PLATFORM BUILDINGS

Ground Plan

REFRESHMENT ROOM

KITCHEN

GENERAL WAITING ROOM

LADIES' WAITING ROOM

W.C.

GENTLEMEN'S TOILET

W C

W C

Side Elevation

GROOMBRIDGE EAST SIGNAL BOX

1 0 1 2 3 4 5 6 7 8 9 10   15   20   25

Scale feet

162

GROOMBRIDGE GOODS WAREHOUSE

Side Elevation (opposite side is of four brick panels as at 'A')

End Elevation (no window at opposite end)

THE BLACKSMITH'S SHOP & STABLE

End Elevation (when in use as a garage)

Front Elevation

End Elevation

1 0 1 2 3 4 5 6 7 8 9 10   15   20   25

Scale feet

SIGNAL BOXES

ERIDGE

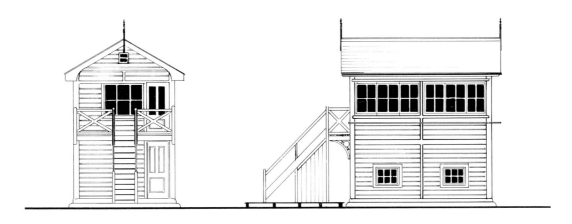

BIRCHDEN JUNCTION

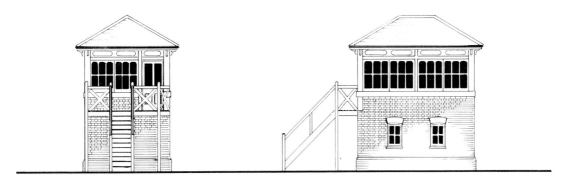

GROOMBRIDGE JUNCTION

164

HEATHFIELD *Outline drawings of the shed used by Glynde Creameries Ltd.* *From drawing No. 16090, dated May 1919*

GROUND PLAN

Existing concrete   New concrete

SOUTH ELEVATION

concrete wall

0 1 2 3 4 5 6 7 8 9 10 11 12 13 14 15
Scale feet

EAST ELEVATION

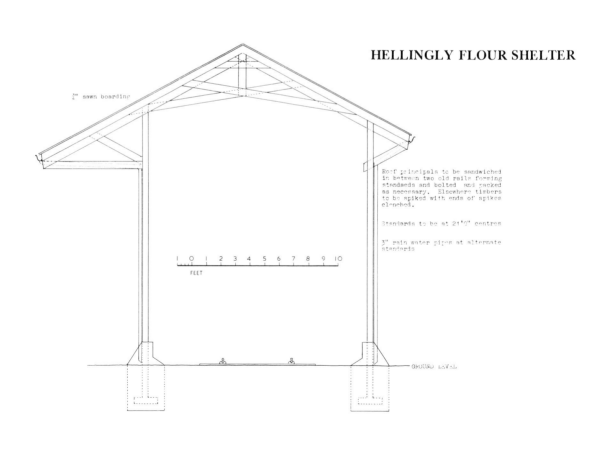

HELLINGLY FLOUR SHELTER

¾" sawn boarding

Roof principals to be sandwiched
in between two old rails forming
standards and bolted and packed
as necessary. Elsewhere timbers
to be spiked with ends of spikes
clenched.

Standards to be at 21'0" centres

3" rain water pipes at alternate
standards

1 0 1 2 3 4 5 6 7 8 9 10
FEET

GROUND LEVEL

HELLINGLY HOSPITAL MOTIVE POWER

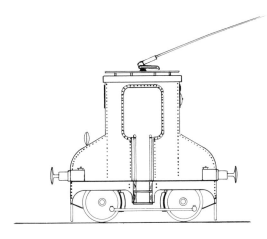
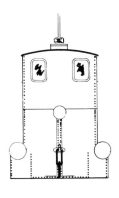

0 1 2 3 4 5 6 7 8 9 10 11 12 13 14 15
Scale feet

LOCOMOTIVE

Length over headstocks	9' 10½"
Width over sills	6' 9½"
Height [rail to roof top]	10' 2"
Wheelbase	5' 6"

TRAMCAR

Length over body	9' 7"
Width over body [at waist]	6' 4½"
Height inside	7' 4"
Wheelbase	5' 6"

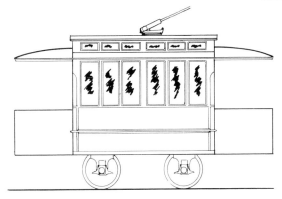

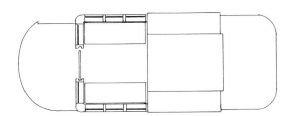

SIGNALLING DIAGRAMS

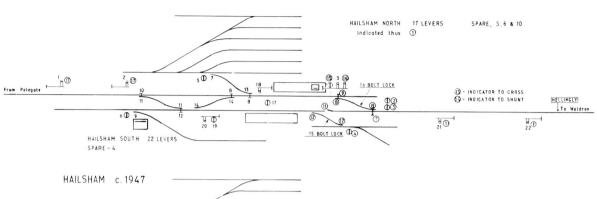

HAILSHAM c.1918

HAILSHAM NORTH 17 LEVERS SPARE, 5, 6 & 10
Indicated thus ①

16 BOLT LOCK

From Polegate

⑬ - INDICATOR TO CROSS
⑭ - INDICATOR TO SHUNT

HELLINGLY
↓ To Waldron

HAILSHAM SOUTH 22 LEVERS
SPARE - 4

15 BOLT LOCK

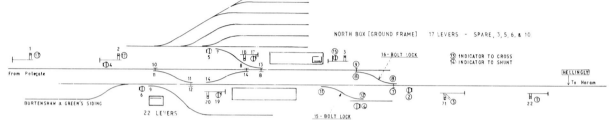

HAILSHAM c.1947

NORTH BOX [GROUND FRAME] 17 LEVERS - SPARE, 3, 5, 6 & 10

16 - BOLT LOCK

From Polegate

⑬ INDICATOR TO CROSS
⑭ INDICATOR TO SHUNT

HELLINGLY
↓ To Horam

BURTENSHAW & GREEN'S SIDING

22 LEVERS

15 - BOLT LOCK

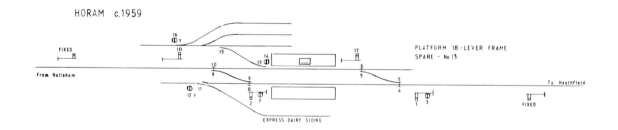

HORAM c.1959

PLATFORM 18-LEVER FRAME
SPARE - No 13

FIXED

From Hailsham

To Heathfield

FIXED

EXPRESS DAIRY SIDING

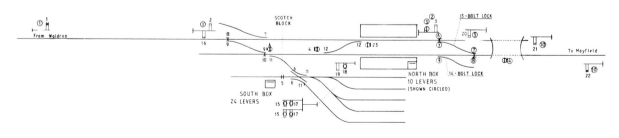

HEATHFIELD c.1920

SCOTCH
BLOCK

13-BOLT LOCK

From Waldron

To Mayfield

NORTH BOX
10 LEVERS
(SHOWN CIRCLED)

14-BOLT LOCK

SOUTH BOX
24 LEVERS

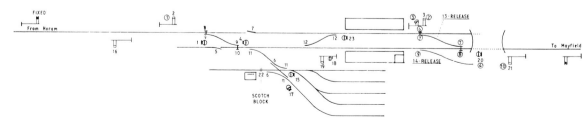

HEATHFIELD c.1965

FIXED

13 - RELEASE

From Horam

To Mayfield

14 - RELEASE

SCOTCH
BLOCK

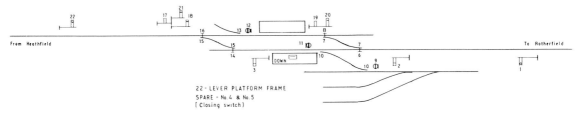

MAYFIELD c.1947

From Heathfield — To Rotherfield

22-LEVER PLATFORM FRAME
SPARE - No.4 & No.5
[Closing switch]

WHEN CLOSED ALL TRAINS USE THE DOWN PLATFORM AND MINIATURE
STAFF TO BE USED FOR THE SECTION BETWEEN HEATHFIELD AND ROTHERFIELD

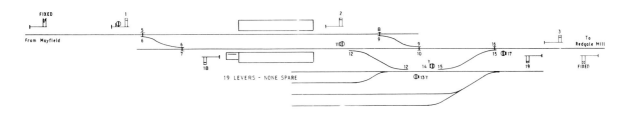

ROTHERFIELD c.1962

FIXED
From Mayfield — To Redgate Mill

19 LEVERS - NONE SPARE

REDGATE MILL JUNCTION SIGNAL DIAGRAMS

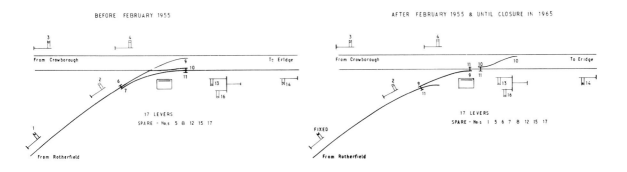

BEFORE FEBRUARY 1955

From Crowborough — To Eridge

From Rotherfield

17 LEVERS
SPARE - No.s 5 8 12 15 17

AFTER FEBRUARY 1955 & UNTIL CLOSURE IN 1965

From Crowborough — To Eridge

From Rotherfield

17 LEVERS
SPARE - No.s 1 5 6 7 8 12 15 17

ERIDGE SIGNALLING c. 1893

Indications of some of the alterations required for the doubling of the line to Uckfield in 1894, are shown.

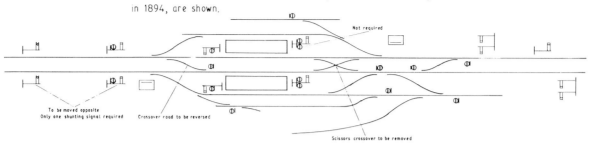

Not required

To be moved opposite
Only one shunting signal required

Crossover road to be reversed

Scissors crossover to be removed

ERIDGE c.1960

SIGNAL DIAGRAMS
(incomplete)

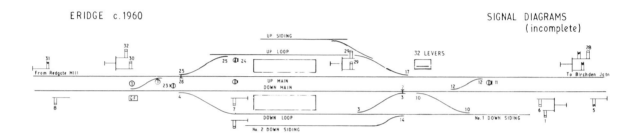

ERIDGE c.1966

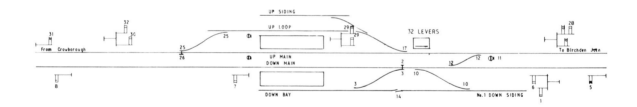

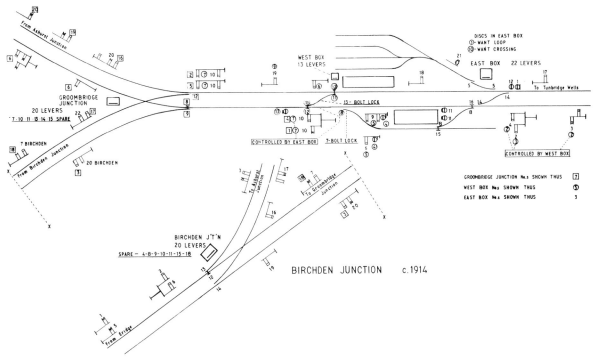

GROOMBRIDGE & GROOMBRIDGE JUNCTION   c.1914

SIGNAL DIAGRAM

BIRCHDEN JUNCTION   c.1914

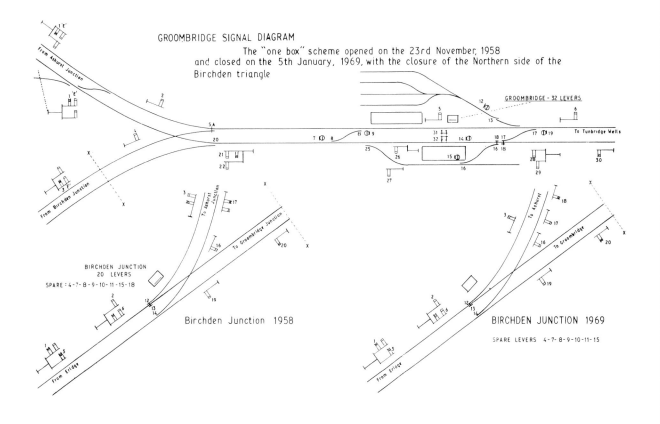

GROOMBRIDGE SIGNAL DIAGRAM

The "one box" scheme opened on the 23rd November, 1958
and closed on the 5th January, 1969, with the closure of the Northern side of the
Birchden triangle

Birchden Junction 1958

BIRCHDEN JUNCTION 1969

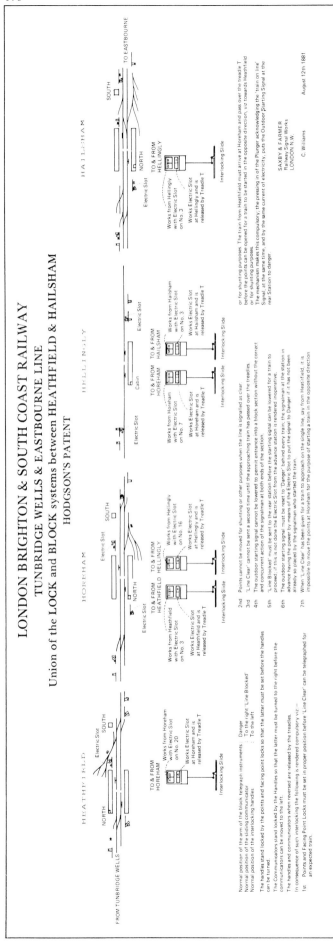

SUMMARY OF CORRESPONDENCE
between SAXBY & FARMER and THE BOARD OF TRADE
from 12th October 1877 to 10th January 1882

On 12th October 1877 Saxby & Farmer wrote to the Board of Trade inviting an inspection of their new arrangement for the mechanical uniting of the Block and the Interlocking systems.

This was acknowledged by the Board of Trade on 15th October and referred to their Inspecting Officers, one of whom, Col. Yolland, acted promptly, and his report dated 22nd October concluded with the words 'There is no doubt that the arrangements, if adopted, would have an important effect in diminishing the number of collisions between trains'.

Saxby & Farmer requested a copy of the report on 26th October and this was sent to them on 30th October with the comment that 'this memo is communicated to you for your private information'.

On 22nd November Saxby & Farmer wrote to the Board of Trade suggesting that the new system should be added to the printed list of requirements for new railways, to which the Board of Trade replied on the following day that they could not include the inventions of private firms but that they would be interested to learn of its use in practice.

A description of the system appeared in *The Times* dated 23rd November 1877, and a copy of this was sent to the Board of Trade who received it on 12th December.

On 13th July 1878 Saxby & Farmer requested a copy of the revised Board of Trade Requirements for New Railways, and this was sent on the following day.

On 1st May 1879 Saxby & Farmer wrote to the Board of Trade commenting on the number of accidents which could have been avoided if their apparatus had been in use, and this letter concluded:

'As to the difficulty of getting such improvements adopted voluntarily the following facts need no comment:- This invention was brought out in January, 1877. In the early part of that year an illustrated explanation of the improvements was sent by post individually to every Railway Director and Principal Officer in the Kingdom and with the result that up to the present time we have not received one single order for it . . . It is however true that the Brighton Railway Company have tested its practicability by allowing it to be worked at one of their stations — at our expense . . . '

This letter was acknowledged on 2nd May with the comment that the Inspecting Officers would not consider further action at that time.

On 8th August 1881 the LBSCR invited the Board of Trade to inspect the use of the Saxby & Farmer system on the Tunbridge Wells line. This was acknowledged on 9th August and Colonel Yolland was appointed to carry out the inspection. Saxby & Farmer sent the Board of Trade a diagram of the system between Heathfield and Hailsham on 12th August and although Col. Yolland's report, dated 25th August, was enthusiastic, the Board of Trade still felt, on 10th January 1882, that further experience was necessary before the system was included as a requirement.